Taking seriously the teachings of the great world religions, Al Truesdale carefully articulates the uniqueness of Christianity's confession of Jesus Christ. The life, death, and resurrection of Jesus are the specifics that Christians teach and proclaim. The triune God witnessed in Scripture sends disciples forth in mission. Beyond religious pluralism Christian witness abides.

Craig L. Nessan, ThD
Professor of Contextual Theology and Ethics
Wartburg Theological Seminary

The Christ follower who accepts a maximal interpretation of the person and work of Christ, in the tradition of historic Christian orthodoxy, has both a daunting challenge and a marvelous opportunity at hand today. The ever more interconnected expressions of faith and culture in a wired world means that we cannot—nor should we—feign ignorance of or express contempt for the great historic faith communities that share the globe with the body of Christ. Human seekers have taken many pathways. We can learn of their convergences with and their divergences from truths we hold dear. We can see them in their nobility and their hypocrisy, just as historic expressions of Christian faith have been both noble and shamefully unchristlike. This is our challenge. But finally, is Jesus Christ "the way, and the truth, and the life," the unique pathway to right relationship with God? Al Truesdale says "yes," unapologetically, and celebrates the fact that a maximal presentation of Christ can respond both sensitively and boldly to the global history of human yearning for truth and life. This is our unique opportunity today.

David L. Wheeler, ThD
Adjunct Professor of Theology, Palmer Theological Seminary
Former Professor of Theology and Ethics, Central Baptist Seminary
Senior Pastor, First Baptist Church of Portland

In a time when the whole notion of *truth* is up for grabs, Al Truesdale gives us a needed defense of the historic Christian commitment to the universal and unique lordship of Christ. Grounded in Scripture and conversant with contemporary scholars, *Confessing Christ as Lord* challenges us to think about our faith with eyes enlightened by the Spirit. This book is readable, fair, and soaked with implications for how the church lives out its faith in a pluralistic context. I strongly recommend it!

Dean Flemming, PhD
Professor Emeritus of New Testament and Mission
MidAmerica Nazarene University
Author, *Foretaste of the Future: Reading Revelation in Light of God's Mission* (IVP Academic, 2022); *Recovering the Full Mission of God: A Biblical Perspective on Being, Doing and Telling* (IVP Academic, 2013)

Can Christians still affirm Jesus Christ as the unique way to God? First reviewing the great world religions, Al Truesdale draws widely on contemporary biblical scholarship to present a comprehensive overview of the Christian claim. This is a critical area in today's multicultural world, and this book is vital reading for pastors and people.

T. A. Noble, PhD
Professor of Theology
Nazarene T
Author, *Holy Trinity: Holy People: The Th*

D1713382

Truesdale's book is an accessible guide to the major world religions as well as the heart of the Christian gospel—the life, death, and resurrection of Messiah Jesus. This is not a polemical attack on other faiths, on the one hand, nor is it one in which Christianity is treated as one amongst many "paths to salvation" on the other. Instead, Truesdale gives a respectful reading of other faiths while maintaining his firm conviction that God's salvation is offered through the life, death, and resurrection of Jesus as the exclusive means of salvation. This book will prove to be valuable for all who wish to have respectful dialogue with their pluralistic friends and neighbors while holding firm to their convictions about the centrality of Christ.

Kent Brower, PhD
Senior Research Fellow in Biblical Studies
Nazarene Theological College (NTC)
Author, *Holiness in the Gospels* (Beacon Hill Press of Kansas City, 2013); *Living as God's Holy People: Holiness and Community in Paul* (Claremont Press, 2020)

In *Confessing Christ as Lord of All in a Pluralistic World*, Al Truesdale has made a timely and compelling case for the distinctive claim of Jesus Christ as Lord of all. His book is unique in that his confidence in the singular lordship of Jesus Christ allows him, first, to present other faith traditions respectfully and accurately, and second, to incorporate much of recent biblical scholarship into his argument. One not only learns what other faith traditions affirm but also learns what makes the Christian faith unique. As one who has had an encounter with the risen Lord, I was grateful to Truesdale for stating so clearly what we who confess Jesus Christ as Lord have discovered. This book will not be one that can be read just once. I know I will return to it again.

Mark Quanstrom, PhD
Director of the Center for Theological Leadership
Northern Seminary
Lisle, Illinois

*Confessing Christ as Lord of All* demonstrates that Christians need not respond to hard questions with timidity but can search for the truth honestly. Amid religious and cultural pluralism, where every system of belief is acknowledged as valid for its adherents, what can Christians say about the special significance of Jesus Christ? Without denigrating other religions, Al Truesdale builds a strong and compelling case for why Jesus can be confessed as Lord of all.

Daryl Ireland, PhD
Administrator, Center for Global Christianity and Mission, Boston University
Principal Investigator, Luce-funded Chinese Christian Poster Project; NEH-funded China Historical Christian Database

# CONFESSING
# CHRIST

*as Lord of All in a Pluralistic World*

## AL TRUESDALE

THE FOUNDRY
PUBLISHING®

The Foundry Publishing®
PO Box 419527
Kansas City, MO 64141
thefoundrypublishing.com

ISBN 978-0-8341-4025-7

Printed in the
United States of America

Cover design: Mike Williams
Interior design: Sharon Page

**Library of Congress Cataloging-in-Publication Data**
A complete catalog record for this book is available from the Library of Congress.

10 9 8 7 6 5 4 3 2 1

To Esther
and God's persecuted church

*The one great Yes of God spoken in Jesus Christ includes both the turning of God to man and that of man to God. In all ages and circumstances this must emerge in every theology.*
—Karl Barth, *Church Dogmatics*, vol. 4, pt. 3.1

*The ultimate reality in the world is the self-giving God revealed in Jesus.*
—N. T. Wright, *History and Eschatology*

# CONTENTS

❖ ❖ ❖

# INTRODUCTION

Throughout human history, many beliefs once firmly held have subsequently been abandoned because of new and better information. Should historic Christian faith be added to the list?

*Once upon a time,* many ancient people believed the earth was a flat disc covered by a solid firmament (dome or tent), supported by mountains rising from the disc's edges. The countless stars were fixed just below the firmament, as were the sun and the moon. Above the firmament there existed an "ocean of heaven" from which rains and floods came to earth through "windows." Above the ocean of heaven was heaven. The earth rested on pillars surrounded by "waters below." Finally, beneath the disc was Hades, the domain of the dead.

Even a minimal understanding of our spherical globe, placed at the right distance from the sun, one tiny member of the Milky Way galaxy, home to billions of stars and their solar systems, shows why an ancient cosmology is completely untenable. The astonishing photograph of the earth—the "blue marble"—taken from Apollo 17 should be sufficient.

*Once upon a time,* people believed diseases were caused by demons or were perhaps inflicted by deities unhappy with human behavior. For many, the concept of an accident—an event not caused by divine action or fate—did not exist.

Today, knowledge of germs, defective organs, viruses, genetic disorders, and environmental influences as causes of disease makes ancient explanations unattractive.

*Once upon a time*, Christians believed that Jesus was the only Savior of the world. They believed that he was God incarnate, the second person of the Trinity, commissioned by the Father to inaugurate the long-anticipated kingdom of God on earth as joyous good news for all people (Luke 4:18; Rom. 1:16). He is, they proclaimed, "Lord of all" (Acts 10:36). Christians believed that to know God truly and live rightly, a person must come to know Jesus as "the way and the truth and the life" (John 14:6) and that such knowledge is "eternal life" (3:16). Christians affirmed that through Christ, all things in heaven and earth were created, that in him all things cohere, and that in him alone God is now reconciling the world to himself (Eph. 1:3-10; Col. 1:15-20). Such claims characterize the New Testament.

All these affirmations are called into question by the impact of modern religious and cultural pluralism. There are numerous ways to define religious pluralism. Here it means affirming the contributions to human flourishing made by all religious traditions and privileging none of them. People just choose to be religious in multiple ways. Lesslie Newbigin, longtime Christian missionary in India, labeled religious pluralism today's "reigning plausibility structure."[1]

In *The Myth of Christian Uniqueness*, an impressive array of Christian thinkers argue that traditional Christian claims about Christ as the world's sole redeemer must be replaced by a theology of religions that recognizes the contributions of all religions. Christ as the "unique" redeemer is a culturally and historically conditioned "myth."[2]

The late Burton L. Mack (d. 2022), John Wesley Professor of Early Christianity at the Claremont School of Theology (California), agreed. In *The Myth of Christian Supremacy*, Mack argued that when we realize Christianity, like all religions, is the result of a long myth-making process, we will understand why Jesus Christ cannot be offered as the world's only redeemer, no more so than any other great religious leader. The world

---

1. Lesslie Newbigin, *The Gospel in a Pluralist Society* (Grand Rapids: Eerdmans, 1989), 169.

2. John Hick and Paul F. Knitter, eds., *The Myth of Christian Uniqueness: Toward a Pluralistic Theology of Religions* (Eugene, OR: Wipf and Stock, 2004).

needs a new common myth composed of the best of all the world's religions and more.[3]

Prominent American theologian David Bentley Hart identifies what he sees as the originating error of traditional Christianity. From the beginning, Christians have absurdly treated a local and limited first-century event in Palestine as containing "the eternal and universal truth of all things."[4] Trying to build an edifice of eternal truth upon a tiny, tenuous, and fleeting episode is "positively absurd."[5]

Distinguished American historian Jon Meacham offers a way to remain "Christian" while denying Christianity's traditional universal claims. In *The Hope of Glory: Reflections on the Last Words of Jesus from the Cross*, Meacham says he "profess[es] the [ecumenical] creeds," confesses his "(many) sins," regularly receives the Holy Eucharist, believes in Jesus's Easter resurrection, and hopes his children will embrace the Christian faith. But he rejects all claims that faith in Jesus is the only path to salvation.[6]

Do these voices provide the only "credible" option for Christians in a pluralistic world? No!

Thanks to the fruitful work of many contemporary biblical scholars, we probably have clearer reasons for confessing Jesus Christ to be the world's redeemer, Lord of all, than at any time since the close of the New Testament era. This book mines the work of some of these scholars and helps equip orthodox Christians with sound reasons for confessing and practicing their faith wherever their places of witness might be.

The book is predicated on New Testament and apostolic affirmations about Jesus of Nazareth: he is "Lord of all" (Acts 10:36), the sovereign *Kyrios*[7] (Rom. 10:9; 1 Cor. 12:3; Phil. 2:11). Jesus is the definitive revela-

---

3. Burton L. Mack, *The Myth of Christian Supremacy: Restoring Our Democratic Ideals* (Minneapolis: Fortress Press, 2022).

4. David Bentley Hart, *Tradition and Apocalypse: An Essay on the Future of Christian Belief* (Grand Rapids: Baker Academic, 2021), 4.

5. Ibid.

6. Jon Meacham, *The Hope of Glory: Reflections on the Last Words of Jesus from the Cross* (New York: Convergent Books, 2020), 7.

7. The word characteristically used in the Septuagint (the Greek version of the Old Testament) to translate the tetragrammaton— that is, the four Hebrew letters used to form the Hebrew name of God, YHWH. When vowels are added, the word becomes YAHWEH.

tion of the one true God and what he is doing in his world.[8] Joseph Cardinal Ratzinger is correct: Dismissing the Christian claim to truth while remaining "Christian," as Jon Meacham does, renounces the "Christian faith itself."[9] The effort is a "beautiful fiction" in a "make-believe world."[10]

The book is arranged in two parts: The *first* provides summaries of six major world religions (Hinduism, Jainism, Buddhism, Sikhism, Judaism, and Islam) and shorter summaries of others (Taoism, Confucianism, Zoroastrianism, Shinto, the Bahá'í Faith). The summaries acquaint readers with the larger religious context within which the Christian faith makes its affirmations and within which religious dialogue occurs. It helps them appreciate the diverse perceptions of reality and human flourishing advanced by other religions.

When considering religions other than one's own, fairness and listening are imperative. A sure way to discredit the Christian faith is to misrepresent another religion. A Christ who could succeed only by misrepresenting or coercing others would be no "savior" at all. The *manner* in which the Christian faith is presented must faithfully express the *character* of the God of grace to whom the gospel bears witness (cf. 2 Cor. 4:1-6).

The *second part* provides conceptual and historical reasons for why the Christian faith affirms Jesus of Nazareth to be the world's redeemer. Chapter 8 examines the primary reason for the Christian confession. Chapter 9 locates the meaning of Jesus's resurrection within the biblical account of the *mission of God*. Chapters 10 and 11 consider the historical reasons for confessing Christ as Lord of all. Chapter 12 listens as the four Gospels narrate the Jesus story. Chapter 13 reflects on how the apostle Paul, major contributor to the New Testament and significant framer of Christian faith, understood his encounter with the risen Christ.

---

8. N. T. Wright, *History and Eschatology: Jesus and the Promise of Natural Theology* (Waco, TX: Baylor University Press, 2019), 74.

9. Benedict XVI (Joseph Cardinal Ratzinger), *Truth and Tolerance: Christian Belief and World Religions*, trans. Henry Taylor (San Francisco: Ignatius Press, 2004), 216.

10. Ibid.

It is not the purpose of this book to examine the relationship between Christianity and other religions.[11] Methodist theologian Geoffrey Wainwright simply advises us to "value the signs of God's saving presence" wherever they may be.[12]

---

11. Many Christians are engaged in developing a theology of religions and in offering an orthodox treatment of religious pluralism. These include Paul Knitter, *Introducing Theologies of Religions* (Maryknoll, NY: Orbis Books, 2002); Veli-Matti Kärkkäinen, *An Introduction to the Theology of Religions: Biblical, Historical and Contemporary Perspectives* (Downers Grove, IL: IVP Academic, 2003); Veli-Matti Kärkkäinen, *Trinity and Religious Pluralism: The Doctrine of the Trinity in Christian Theology of Religions* (Burlington, VT: Ashgate, 2004); Harold Netland, *Dissonant Voices: Religious Pluralism and the Question of Truth* (Vancouver, BC: Regent College Publishing, 1991); Harold Netland, *Encountering Religious Pluralism: The Challenge to Christian Faith and Mission* (Downers Grove, IL: IVP Academic, 2001); Gerald McDermott, *Can Evangelicals Learn from World Religions? Jesus, Revelation and Religious Transitions* (Downers Grove, IL: IVP, 2000); Joseph Cardinal Ratzinger, *Truth and Tolerance: Christian Belief and World Religions*, trans. Henry Taylor (San Francisco: Ignatius Press, 2004); Bryan Stone, *Evangelism after Pluralism: The Ethics of Christian Witness* (Grand Rapids: Baker Academic, 2018); and Al Truesdale with Keri Mitchell, *With Cords of Love: A Wesleyan Response to Religious Pluralism* (Kansas City: Beacon Hill Press of Kansas City, 2006).

12. Geoffrey Wainwright, *Doxology: The Praise of God in Worship, Doctrine, and Life* (New York: Oxford University Press, 1980), 385.

# PART I
## *Summaries of Other World Religions*

# 1
# HINDUISM

The religious beliefs and practices known as Hinduism, largely associated with India, are immensely diverse.

There is no "orthodoxy," no system of doctrine, no universal "creed" by which one can be judged a "true Hindu."[1] Belief options range from polytheism (many gods) to atheism. Options for practice run from strict asceticism (severe self-discipline) to active life in the world. A Hindu may regularly worship in a temple, or never go. The only universal rule is that one live strictly by the rules and rituals of the version of Hinduism embraced, and trust by doing so their next birth will improve over the current one. All "approved" forms of Hinduism lead to achieving that goal.

---

1. Currently this assessment is being challenged by champions of Hindutva ("Hindu-ness"), Sanskrit for the essence of being Hindu. Hindutva is a political ideology that claims India as a predominantly Hindu nation. The ideology expands to include minority faiths rooted in India, such as Sikhism, Jainism, and Buddhism. Hindutva promotes right-wing Hindu nationalism. By contrast, others describe Hindutva as an ideology that "brings everyone together, unites everyone within itself, and makes everyone prosper" (Suhag Shukla, "What Does Hindutva Really Mean?", Hindu American Foundation, Oct. 5, 2021, https://www.hinduamerican .org/blog/what-does-hindutva-mean).

Hinduism is best thought of as a "family of religions."[2] It "comprehends the living faiths of the peoples of India who call themselves Hindus."[3]

# Early Hinduism

Early Hinduism is characterized by moving from ritual sacrifice to a hunger for release from the Law of Karma, and union with what is ultimately real.

## The Vedic Age (c. 2500–600 BC)

About the second millennium BC, waves of warlike people of Indo-European background arrived in northwest India. They called themselves Aryans. Scholars refer to them as Indo-Aryans. For centuries they poured over the passes of the Hindu Kush Mountains. In time they migrated further into India and began living in simple village groups. As they advanced, they overcame the black-skinned Dravidians who occupied the land before them. They also fought among themselves in intertribal conflict. These clashes were later immortalized in two Hindu epics, the Ramayana and the Mahabharata.

Tribes were ruled by kings or chieftains known as rajahs. A rajah maintained an army of priests who sought divine blessings for the rajah and his people. Eventually the priests developed prayers and hymns to be celebrated by the people.

As the Aryans settled, so did their migratory adventures. But they retained adventurous wanderings through imagination. Their past was lived orally through folktales and epic accounts. Ritual sacrifices became more complex.

Hymns and prayers expanded religious perceptions. From them came the earliest sacred texts (2000-1000 BC), the four Samhitas (collections): the Rig-Veda, Sama-Veda (sacred knowledge), Yajur-Veda, and Atharva-Veda. They reveal an exuberant people who faced life confidently. The Indo-Aryan gods largely derive from the four Vedas. Each Veda was later

---

2. John B. Noss, *Man's Religions*, 7th ed. (New York: Macmillan, 1984), 72. For a collection of readings from the world's religions, see Philip Novak, *The World's Wisdom: Sacred Texts of the World's Religions* (San Francisco: HarperSanFrancisco, 1994).

3. Noss, *Man's Religions*, 72.

supplemented by one or more Brahmanas—directions for the proper ritual use of Vedic hymns and prayers. Brahmanas were supplemented by the Aranyakas or Forest Books. They explained how people who retired to the forests were to use the hymns and prayers. From the Forest Books emerged the famous Upanishads—philosophical discussions to guide all thought and action.

The Rig-Veda (the Veda of stanzas of praise) contains religious poetry in ten books. The Rig-Veda reveals the religious devotion of family before and during the Vedic Age. High flights of poetry praise the deities. The hymns are prayers addressed to one or more deities, called "devas" or "shining ones." When worshipping, the Aryans approached the altar joyously and confidently. Having no temples, they worshipped under the open sky. Sacrificial offerings ranged from melted butter to costly horses. Over time the priests' assignments became more complex and delineated. The most important priest became the Brahmin or presiding priest. He represented the central sacred petition or Brahman (the prayer, holy word, incantation, sacred knowledge, etc.).

From the sacrificial rituals emerged an ever-expanding mythology explaining the origin of all things. Gods were reconceived and given new powers. Older gods faded and more powerful gods replaced them. Divine powers such as Agni, Soma, and Brihaspati were introduced into the rituals. New cosmic gods were introduced when it was realized the whole world was included and affected by the rituals.

Prominent among the gods of the Rig-Veda was blustering Indra. He was ruler of the gods of the mid-region of the sky, especially the god of storms. Indra was also the god of war. He shouted and roared with a loud voice. To his worshippers Indra appeared with long-flowing hair and a wind-tossed beard. With an enemy-destroying thunderbolt in his hand, Indra smote the drought-dragon holding back the mountain waters needed for planting and vegetation. Indra's prominence should not be mistaken as monotheism. During their prayers, Aryans spoke of each major deity as supreme.

In sharp contrast to Indra stood the feared and puzzling mountain god Rudra. Rudra was author of destructive storms that swept down from the Himalayas. He destroyed goods and persons. Rudra was approached in humility and trembling, beseeching him to be merciful. However, at times Rudra became a gentle healer. In his mountain fortress, Rudra presided over medicinal plants. He is the early form of the "great god" Shiva, Destroyer and Reviver (whom we shall meet later).

Another deity in the Rig-Veda, whose importance will eventually extensively increase, is the far-striding Vishnu. Vishnu encompasses the earth, atmosphere, and sky in three swift strides. He redeems the world from night and preserves the world's being. Rudra and Vishnu will surpass the minor Vedic deities (e.g., Agni, the god of the altar-fire who drove away the demons; Soma, the divine presence in the intoxicating juice of the soma plant; and Brihaspati known to the priests as the holy power in their prayers) to become major Hindu gods.

Morally far above all other gods stood the awe-inspiring Varuna. He directed the forces that promoted ritual, natural, and moral order. Varuna upheld the world's physical order. He revealed sin, was the judge of truth and falsehood, kept people obedient to the moral law, and forgave sins.

Yama, the first man to die, became the god of the dead, judge and ruler of the departed.

The other Vedas are largely dependent, even appendages, of the Rig-Veda. The Yajur-Veda provided material for devotional use of the Rig-Veda. The Sama-Veda is a collection of rhythmic chants for use by priests. The Atharva-Veda is a treasury of charms, incantations, and ancient spells. They give expression to fear, passion, hate, physical distress, and tell how to gain relief.

Toward the close of the Vedic Age there appeared a yearning for assurance of unity in the totality of all things. One hymn is addressed to "that one thing," a principle whose existence preceded the universe. The hymn shows the priests were exhibiting philosophical interests in the origin of all things and wondering if it has a name.

## Brahmanism

*Rise of the Caste System.* By the end of the seventh century BC, distinct principalities or states and four distinct social groups had developed (1) the nobles (Kshatriyas), (2) the priests (Brahmins), (3) the Aryan common people (the Vaisyas), and (4) and the enslaved non-Aryan Blacks

(Shudras). More and more the first three classes held themselves aloof from the Shudras. The question of "color"—*varna*, the Hindu word for caste—had surfaced. Sharp social separations between the first three and the fourth classifications were established. There also existed a struggle for social prestige between ruling nobles and Brahmins. Each one claimed superiority. High regard for the Brahmins, keepers of holy power in sacrificial prayers, eclipsed the nobles, as their importance as warriors declined. Priests occupied the central place of power.

*The Brahmanas* (first written c. 300 BC). To each Veda there was attached one or more Brahmanas. They were textbooks of the various schools of Brahmins. The priests were fascinated by the process of interpreting their rituals. They could cause events to happen. Sacrifices could serve either domestic or public purposes. Throughout the directions contained in the Brahmanas there is an increasing spiritual aspiration and a growing sense of a single principle of unity in the universe.

## The Philosophy of the Upanishads (800-600 BC)

The six systems of Hindu philosophy have their origin in this era. The question, "Could the holy power at work in the prayer formulas—Brahman—be the ultimate eternal power of the universe?" introduces one of the most speculative eras in the history of religion.

Thoughts of alert minds are embedded in the Upanishads ("sittings near a teacher"), which are appendages to the Vedas. In them, all classes, including women, take part in the dialogues. Two tendencies are apparent. The *first* is to move away from activity in the world and toward contemplation in mind and spirit. The number of ascetics and brooding thinkers was increasing. Even priests (Brahmins) were retiring to the forests to practice meditation. Give up the world and seek emancipation (moksha) from its illusions and pains. The *second* was to react against ritualism without abandoning it. The intent was to find equivalents in ascetic acts of mind and body. The wisdom of sages became valued. The heat that fires the ascetic in the forest is equivalent to the fire on the altar. Mental repetition of Vedic chants is equal to reciting them before the altar. Sacrifice within oneself is equal to sacrificing to the gods.

An increasing emphasis upon one's inner self (atman) emerges. "Compared with this inner self the natural world (*prakriti*, matter), including the body and its sensory and mental states, is of an inferior order." To "choose to ignore the inner self and be content with the natural world would be an act of ignorance that could only result in illusion and suffering."[4] To attain salvation, it is best to "break away from the natural world and from one's sensory and mental experience in it, through asceticism and meditation."[5]

Some Upanishads would settle for a sharp dualism, a separation, between the world (*prakriti*), and spirit or soul (atman). Other Upanishads offered a unified position (known in philosophy as monism, only a single reality). They find identical unity and sameness everywhere. For example, the fire in the sun is identical with the creative power of being itself. All things are essentially equivalent. Many Upanishads say Brahman (the objective All, the Objective Self) and atman (the inner self, the soul) are identical. The objective and the subjective are one, seen from two perspectives. *Tat tvam asi*, "That are thou." The all-Soul is "the very stuff of which the human soul is formed."[6]

Everything, including the gods, is derived by self-distribution from one original source. Ultimately, all things are bound together in essence, in being. Separateness is an illusion; all-inclusive Being is real. The person who learns this will seek deliverance (moksha) from the illusion of separateness through mystical union with Being. A name for this *unity* is Brahman. Brahman is sometimes spoken of as personal, sometimes as impersonal, sometimes as having attributes, sometimes as not (Nirguna Brahman), sometimes as knowable (Saguna Brahman), sometimes as unknowable. All things, all creatures, are ultimately phases of *That One.*

Finally, "When the human soul *knows* its complete identity with *Brahman*, it celebrates with a feeling of unity approaching ecstasy."[7] The highest state of *knowing* is Pure Consciousness. It involves union with Brahman (called *turiya* or *caturtha*). Brahman and atman become indis-

---

4. Ibid., 86.
5. Ibid.
6. Ibid., 88.
7. Ibid.

tinguishable, held together in their pure single essence. It is more correct to say Brahma-atman without any reservations.

## Reincarnation and the Law of Karma

During this period (800-600 BC) belief in reincarnation and karma—two factors that became central elements in Hinduism—appeared.

Belief in the transmigration of souls or reincarnation (known as samsara) means the soul of a person who dies will not normally pass into a permanent state such as heaven or hell. Instead, the soul is reborn into another existence. There will be subsequent rebirths. One exception is the soul of one who at death returns to indistinguishable oneness with Brahman. This is the goal of all rebirths. Each rebirth might become a form of life higher or lower than the previous one. But what determines one's next birth? The Law of Karma.

The Law of Karma focuses on ethical consequences of one's thoughts, words, and deeds. They determine the form of one's future existence. Impersonal, the Law operates like a law of nature. Karma is the *cause* of what is now happening in one's life. Deeds shape character and soul. In its most rigid form, the Law of Karma "implies that everything a man does, each separate deed of life, weighed along with every other deed, determines destiny."[8]

Some Hindus reinterpret the Law to mean a person "reaps what he sows." The discouragement, unhappiness, and emotional revulsion the Law of Karma produces are not surprising. Even the enjoyment of desires may be harmful. One Upanishad text says, "In this cycle of existence I am like a frog in a waterless well."[9]

The caste system, once so distinctive of Hinduism, can be understood in light of the Law of Karma. The order was: first the Brahmins, next the Kshatriyas (nobles), then the dependent Vaisyas or "vassals," and finally the Shudras or servants. Outside the caste system were the out-castes, the untouchables (now known as Dalits, "oppressed")[10]—the dregs of society. They had no hope of ever advancing in the social scale. In centuries after

---

8. Ibid., 90.

9. Ibid., 91.

10. Article 17 of India's Constitution bans the practice of untouchability. But that hasn't ended its practice. Despite laws enacted to protect Dalits, they still face widespread discrimina-

c. 500 BC, lines were drawn within the caste system. Subsequently, caste distinctions fissured into hundreds of sub-castes, each forbidding inter-marriage.

The caste into which a person was born was the result of the Law of Karma. A person born a Shudra might have sinned in a previous life and now deserves what he has received. Someone who is now a Brahmin lived well in his previous life; he deserves his present privileges. The morally accomplished should be on top. Attempting to change one's social location is to defy the inexorable Law of Karma.

Hindus began to speak of samsara (reincarnation) as "the Wheel" that eternally revolved. Hearts responded in dread of being bound to "the Wheel," the inflexible Law of Karma, for a possible thousand million rebirths.

For Hindus (and Buddhists) the world's existence is divided into kalpas (aeons). At the end of each kalpa, the world begins again. Each kalpa lasts 4.32 billion years and is divided into fourteen periods.

A reader might ask, "Is there no way of release?" Yes.

# Later Hinduism

Later Hinduism is characterized by practical ways of release from "the Wheel." John Noss observes Hindus "seemed endlessly hospitable to good ideas."[11] That attitude, along with the inclusiveness and tolerance of the Brahmins in addressing needs of the common people, eventuated in the dharma (darma),[12] the approved Hindu way of life that provides paths leading to release from the "Wheel." The dharma includes four permissible goals in life and three paths to salvation.

## The Four Permissible Goals in Life

The four permissible goals in life are the desire for kama, artha, dharma, and moksha.

---

tion. Approximately 15 percent of the Indian population is restricted to the margins of society because of untouchability.

11. Noss, *Man's Religions*, 178.

12. The term has multiple meanings, depending on whether it is being used in Hinduism, Buddhism, or Jainism. For Hinduism "dharma" means religious and moral law that governs one's conduct.

Kama is the desire for pleasure. It is so great that some Hindus regard it as the presence of the god Kama (or Kamadeva), the god of erotic love and pleasure. He is depicted as a handsome youth accompanied by heavenly nymphs. Kama carries a flowery bow with five flower-arrows that can pierce the heart and fill it with desire.

Seeking pleasure is commendable for its vitality and purpose. There is guidance in how to fulfill the desire for pleasure. If one seeks to understand the art of love, it can be found in Vatsyayana's *Kamasutra*, a guide in the art of living well. If one's interest is in the literary arts, guidance will be found in the *Natyasastras*, a detailed treatise on classical dramatic art. If a person's goal is pleasure, established social rules must be followed. Nevertheless, in this or some future existence a pleasure seeker will become awakened to the fact that pleasure does not fulfill. Something more satisfying is needed.

Artha involves desire for material possessions. Ultimately it is a desire for high social position and success. Though a legitimate goal, this requires a person to be coldhearted and tenacious. Ancient Hindu literature such as the *Arthasatras* and the *Panchatantra* will teach one how to practice ruthless competition. The *Panchatantra* contains animal fables that glorify shrewdness and cleverness.

No shame should be leveled at persons who pursue wealth and power. However, either in this life or some future reincarnation, those who pursue material possessions and influence will discover their emptiness. They will see that true happiness comes by following the path of renunciation.

Dharma establishes criteria for a more worthy and satisfying life. Narrowly, dharma is the religious and moral law that governs individual conduct. It includes truthfulness, non-injury, and generosity. Those who abide by dharma will perform their duty to family, caste, and community. *The Laws of Manu*, a code of conduct for domestic, social, and religious life, will teach people how to renounce selfish pursuit of pleasure, wealth, and social success. They will learn the laws and customs applicable to each caste, and experience joy. But joy that results from obeying dharma, however great, is finally inadequate and temporary. There is only one ultimate satisfaction.

"Moksha" means salvation or release and is ultimately the only satisfying goal in life. Negatively, it means liberation from the "Wheel," the cycle of rebirth and all the physical and spiritual miseries of life. Positively, "moksha" means deliverance into the fullness of being in nirvana. Words cannot adequately express the full meaning and experience of such liberation.

## The Three Ways to Achieve Moksha

*First*, the way of works (the karma yoga [to connect, a yoke, union, team, work]). This is the path of action or deeds. It involves acting in strict compliance with the dharma applicable to a person's station in life, such as the dharma found in *The Laws of Manu* (c. 200 BC). The way of works includes adherence to ritual. It is followed by most Hindus. Karma yoga has the advantage of being practical and understandable and of enjoying the blessing of antiquity. It is not particularly emotional, intellectual, or methodical. "Karma yoga is the path of dedicated work." Consider "the results of our actions as a spiritual offering rather than hoarding the results for ourselves."[13]

The Brahmanas taught that each person owes to the gods sacrifices that are good works par excellence. One owes to these teachers the study of the Vedas. The ancestral spirits are owed offspring and one's fellow humans are owed hospitality.

*Second*, the way of knowledge (*Jnana Marga*). This way is based on the reasoning of the Upanishads and the Hindu philosophic systems. Its premise is that the cause of human misery and evil is ignorance. Human actions have the wrong orientation. Mental error, not moral transgression, is the root of human misery. Release from ignorance and achieving moksha (deliverance) comes through mental and ascetic disciplines.

Ignorance addressed by way of knowledge is that humans persist in thinking they are real, separate selves (atman) distinct from Brahmin when in fact Brahmin-atman is the sole reality. As long as people continue to act ignorantly, they will be endlessly miserable, entangled in succeeding rebirths.

---

13. "The Path of Work: Karma Yoga," the Vedanta Society of Southern California. https://vedanta.org/yoga-spiritual-practice/the-path-of-work-karma-yoga/.

Salvation comes through right understanding. Knowledge that all illusion has ceased, that one has reached a state of consciousness where karma ceases to produce rebirths occurs in an ecstatic flash of certitude during deep meditation. One is admitted into the realm of reality. Union with, absorption into, the infinite has happened. Reaching this goal requires years of preparation and self-discipline, and after going through stages of life that terminate in the life of a hermit, a *sannyasin* or mendicant (beggar) "holy man."

*Third*, the way of devotion (bhakti ["devotional service"] yoga). The way of devotion involves "ardent and hopeful devotion to a particular deity in grateful recognition of aid received or promised. It often assumes the form of a passionate love of the deity, whether god or goddess."[14] Bhakti yoga requires surrender of one's self to the god or goddess through acts of devotion in temple worship and private life. Such devotion leads to salvation (moksha).

Bhakti yoga as a true path to salvation appears in the Bhagavad-Gita or Song of the Blessed Lord (part of the Mahabharata). In it Lord Krishna, the supreme beloved, throws wide open the gate of the way of devotion and invites all wayfarers, no matter their gender or caste, to enter.[15] "Be certain none can perish [while] trusting Me!"[16]

## The Great Triad of Gods

Gradually, three great Hindu gods absorbed the roles of scores of other Hindu deities. The *first* is Brahma, the Creator. He is least widely worshipped and is probably no longer active on earth. *Second*, Shiva, the "great god" (Mahadeva), can be both destructive and auspicious because he plays a constructive and helpful role. Shiva is associated with reproduction in all aspects of life. He has numerous consorts. *Third*, Vishnu, the "preserver," perfectly exhibits winsome love. He is benevolent and the conserver of values. Shiva has numerous avatars, or forms of existence, such as Rama and Krishna.

---

14. Noss, *Man's Religions*, 184.
15. Ibid., 188.
16. Ibid.

## Folk or Popular Hinduism

Eighty percent of India's 1.417 billion citizens are Hindus. A large part of those who are classified as "Hindu" practice folk or popular Hinduism. Folk Hinduism is highly polytheistic. It does not abide by the well-defined classifications we have discussed. Ordinary Hindu villagers aren't interested in making such sharp distinctions. "Most people in India practice orthodox Hinduism conjointly with the primitive forms of religion common to their locality."[17] Worship of the great Hindu gods with proper ritual observance "might exist side by side with wayside stones, trees, or small shrines sacred to village godlings and spirits."[18]

The masses of India's Hindus "go about being religious in the manner that has been traditional in their localities." In their rituals and beliefs, they may observe demonolatry, animal veneration, and devotion to village spirits and godlings.[19] This may or may not be accompanied by worship of major Hindu deities.[20] Ordinary villagers are content to worship the village godlings. They look to these godlings to provide rain, bountiful harvests, and protection from life's endless threats. They may give little thought to reincarnation.

---

17. Ibid., 194.
18. Ibid.
19. Ibid.
20. Ibid.

# 2
# JAINISM (Jain Dharma)

After wandering twelve years, the crowning experience happened to the prophet Mahavira (c. 540-c. 468 BC). During the thirteenth year, while in a squatting position, knees high, and head low, in deep meditation Mahavira reached nirvana, the complete and full release called kevala (moksha). His residue of karma had burned away. He was released from cycles of rebirth. He thus became the Jina, the conqueror.

## Mahavira's Way of Life

Jains believe the roots of their religion reach much deeper than Mahavira. They believe he was the last in a long line of twenty-four earlier prophets (Tirthankaras, "ford finders"), the first of which was Rishabhdev, who lived centuries earlier.

Mahavira means "great man" or "hero." Mahavira's original name was Netaputta Vardhamana. Tradition holds that Mahavira was born near Vaisali in modern Bihar, a state in eastern India. He was reared in luxury by five nurses that characterized ancient Indian courts. He married and had a daughter but was not satisfied with life as a prince.

In a park outside town lived a group of ascetic monks who followed the rule of Parshva, or Parshvanatha, who three centuries earlier had renounced the world. Mahavira was determined to join them. But out of respect for his parents, he waited. After their deaths he prepared by giving away his gold and silver. He removed his ornaments, retained only one robe, and pulled out his hair in five handfuls. Now about age thirty, Mahavira retired from the world, joined the monks, and took the vow of renunciation.

Months later, Mahavira struck out by himself. In summer and winter, he went about naked. For a long time, he wandered in search of release from the cycle of reincarnation. He was driven by two convictions: (1) saving one's soul from evil—expelling contaminating matter—requires severe asceticism, and (2) maintaining purity of soul requires practicing *ahimsa*, or non-injury to any living thing.

After traveling for some time with Goshala, another naked ascetic, Mahavira went his own way and avoided attachment to individuals, groups, or places that might bind him to this world's pleasures.

The "Venerable One," the "houseless one," wandered about, injuring nothing, and begging for food that he ate only after examining it to be sure there were no eggs, sprouts, or worms. He carried a soft broom to remove insects from his pathway. He would not even harm by scratching the insects that crawled over him. He strained his drinking water. Before retiring for the evening, he meticulously cleared his surroundings. His goal was to achieve moksha, deliverance.

After achieving kevala, moksha, full release, Mahavira began to teach others. Conversions continued for the next thirty years. Through the rite of voluntary self-starvation (*sallakhana*) Mahavira finally cut all ties to birth, old age, and death. Now, according to Jains, Mahavira enjoys supreme bliss in Isatpragbhara, a place of reward.

## The Philosophy and Ethics of Jainism

Jains believe humans, in their pursuit of salvation (moksha), are gravely conditioned by the Law of Karma. There are at least eight classes of Karma.[1] Consequences of one's actions are literally deposited in and on one's soul. Karma accumulates in layers that "fix one's lot in each exis-

---

1. See "Types of Karma," The Jain Universe. https://jaincosmos.blogspot.com/2011/05/types-of-karma.html.

tence and affect the whole course of life."[2] The layers must be worn off by the soul's activity.

Matter is non-living substance (*ajiva dravya*). It ranges in density from solid (heavier) to thin (light). Matter is eternal. It may cluster in any shape (e.g., earth, water, living bodies, and the senses). Karma-matter sticks to the soul through bad desire or passion. The soul carries forward all accumulated karma. It can sink lower or rise higher. If light enough, the soul might rise up to heaven and become embodied in some god. If lighter, the soul might become an eternally "liberated" being.

Jains group all things into two categories: (1) ajiva, or lifeless things, especially thick dead matter. It is eternal, yet evil, and (2) jiva, or living beings, understood as the infinite multitude of individual souls composing the realm of spirit (or living substance). They are indestructible and classed according to their number of senses. Jiva is eternal and of infinite value. Jiva contains all good.

When liberated from matter, souls are perfect. They possess infinite perception, knowledge, power, and bliss. They rise to the top of the universe, enter Isatpragbhara, the highest celestial heaven, and do not lose consciousness. Such souls are neither long nor short, neither heavy nor light. Though without a body, souls still retain consciousness.

According to Jain doctrine, salvation is self-contained. Praying to the gods is futile. Other people, including priests, are futile. The Vedas are not magic. Let each person realize that salvation resides within. "Thou are thine own friend," Mahavira taught. The surest path to reach liberation is to practice asceticism or austerities (*tapas*). Jains have added fasting, and meditations that can lead to total dissociation from the outer world and transcendence over one's own physical state. This requires severe control of mind and passions. Preventing new karma from forming through disciplined activity requires that the mind be controlled and cleansed of all love or dependence upon the world.

According to Jain doctrine, right knowledge, right faith, and right conduct are necessary for attaining liberation. To accomplish these essentials, one must observe the "Five Great Vows" (Vratas).

2. Noss, *Man's Religions*, 99.

*First*, ahimsa. Renounce all killing of living things. "Do not injure, abuse, oppress, enslave, insult, torment, torture, or kill any creature or living being."[3] All living creatures are equal. No living creature has a right to harm, injure, or kill any other living being. Ahimsa is the cardinal principle of Jainism and is known as the Jain cornerstone.

*Second*, commit to truth-telling by renouncing all vices and lies. Only if one has conquered greed, fear, anger, jealousy, egoism, and foolishness can one speak the truth.

*Third*, renounce stealing, taking anything not given. A Jain must be totally honest.

*Fourth*, renounce all sexual pleasure. It involves abstention from sensual pleasure and the pleasure of all five senses. This vow is difficult to observe. In marriage, the relationship with one's spouse should be limited.

*Fifth*, renounce all attachments whether little or much, small or great, living or lifeless. Attachment to worldly objects results in bondage to cycles of birth and death. Strict adherence to the five vows is required of all Jain monks and nuns.

Adherence to the Five Great Vows is difficult or impossible for householders or laypersons. Laypersons make twelve vows of laity. They are: limited nonviolence, limited truthfulness, limited non-stealing, limited chastity, limited non-attachment, limited area of activity, limited use of consumable and non-consumable items, limited meditation, limited duration of activity, limited ascetic's life, charity.[4] In general, Jain monks and laypersons are not sharply distinguished.

## Jain Sects and Scripture

Jains are divided into two major sects: (1) the Digambara (meaning "sky-clad," "naked"), and (2) the Svetambara (meaning "white-clad"). Each is divided into subgroups. The two sects agree on the basic principles of Jainism but disagree regarding details of Mahavira's life, the spiritual status of women, ritual, whether monks should wear clothes, and which

---

3. "The Five Maha-vratas (Great Vows) of Ascetics," JAINA: Federation of Jain Associations in North America, https://www.jaina.org/page/FiveMahaVratas.

4. McKenzie Perkins, "Jainism Beliefs: The Five Great Vows and the Twelve Vows of Laity," Learn Religions, https://www.learnreligions.com/jainism-beliefs-vows-4583994.

texts should be accepted as scripture. The Digambara sect is more severe. The Svetambara sect admits women to their monastic order and believes women can experience moksha. According to the Digambara sect, women cannot achieve moksha until they have been reborn as men. Women are not admitted to their temples. They believe Mahavira taught that women are the greatest temptation in the world, the cause of sinful acts.

Jain scriptures are called agamas. Jains believe the agamas were formed by the Tirthankaras and were orally transmitted from one generation to the next. The agamas are divided into two streams: Arthagamas (sermons of the twenty-four Tirthankaras) and Sutragamas (sutras [concise verses] written over the Arthagamas). Digambara believe the original agamas were lost ages ago. Svetambara believe they possess the original texts.

# 3
# BUDDHISM

◈ ◈ ◈

## Gautama's Early Life

Siddhartha (given name) Gautama (family name), founder of Buddhism, was born in 563 BC in northern India to Hindu parents. His father was a petty chieftain who hoped his son would become a universal monarch. At Gautama's birth, soothsayers predicted he might someday abandon home and inheritance to become a monk. Gautama's father was determined to guard against such a calamity.

Though reared in luxury, Gautama had a sensitive spirit accompanied by an analytic mind. Privilege offered no resolution for his restless spirit.

According to tradition, at age sixteen or nineteen, Gautama married a beautiful, graceful princess. But even marriage could not calm his restless spirit. In his twenties, he secretly decided to abandon privilege and adopt the life of a religious mendicant (beggar). After the birth of a son, Rahula, Gautama felt free to follow his secret commitment.

## The "Four Passing Sights"

Buddhists speak of the "Four Passing Sights" as immediate reasons for Gautama becoming a mendicant. To make sure he would become a universal monarch and never a monk, Gautama's father took every precaution against his son experiencing the sorrows of the outside world. He protected his son against observing the solemnities of old age, disease, and death. Surrounded only by youthful attendants, Gautama grew up in ignorance of sorrows common to everyone.

But the gods intervened. One day a god appeared by the roadside in the form of an aged and feeble man. "What is this miserable sight?" Gautama asked. His charioteer explained that old age is the lot of all people. On another day, a god appeared as a loathsomely diseased person. Shaken by this new sight, Gautama learned physical illness and misery can fall upon anyone, regardless of social position. On a subsequent day, Gautama saw a corpse being taken for burial. Robbed of peace of mind, Gautama painfully learned about the end of life for all. In horror, he learned illness and death would be his lot as well. His joy expired.

When the fourth sight occurred, Gautama saw a calm ascetic clothed in a yellow robe. He had obtained peace of mind. From the monks, Gautama hoped to learn how to gain freedom over fear of old age, disease, and death.

## The Great Renunciation

Gautama's father ordered dancing girls to entertain his son to overcome his melancholy. After the dancers had fallen exhausted, in disgust Gautama stepped over their sprawled bodies. He went to the quarters of his sleeping wife and son, bade them an unspoken farewell, and went out into the world to pursue peace of mind. He shaved his head and beard and exchanged his elegant robe for a coarse yellow robe. He then plunged into the forest.

## The Six Years of Quest

For six years, Gautama sought peace by way of Hindu Brahmin philosophy. In search of enlightenment, he attached himself to a series of Hindu teachers. Disappointed, he withdrew and began unsuccessfully to follow the extreme asceticism of the Jains.

Abandoning the Jains, Gautama wandered, and eventually entered a grove of trees at Uruvela. Sitting there he practiced such intense self-discipline that he almost died. He believed the mind would become clear as the body became more disciplined. Accounts of his self-denial include eating nauseous food, sitting on thorns, and wearing irritating garments. But no form of austerity could deliver understanding. He was as far from success as ever. Self-mortification had failed. Could there be a successful path?

# The Great Enlightenment

Six years of searching had failed. Gautama took his begging bowl and resumed the life of a wandering beggar. One day he came to a grove and sat under a fig tree. The tree came to be known as the Bo-tree, or Knowledge tree. He resolved not to leave until achieving enlightenment.

Suddenly the answer came. His suffering was due to desire (*tanha*, "thirst," "craving"). His entire life had been lived in "desire." But what causes ensnaring desire? Gautama determined to find the causes, and also how to prevent craving from arising. If resolved, Gautama could assist others.

To prevent enlightenment from happening, Mara, the Evil One, the god of desire and death, in an awful struggle, tried to convince Gautama to abandon his quest. In the end, Gautama prevailed, and Mara fled.[1] Shortly thereafter, full enlightenment, *Bodhi* came. Gautama was transported into a new life, free from desire and pain. He was purged of wrong states of mind. For him, rebirth would be no more. He had experienced the earthly foretaste of nirvana (nibbana).

Gautama was now the Buddha, the Enlightened One.

But immediately there arose a problem. Were he to announce his insight (his dharma), and were others not to understand or reject, he would have fallen back into his old state of desire and frustration. Should he remain alone "enlightened," or should he teach others? After exhausting his karma, should he wait to enter nirvana at death, or should he postpone that goal and become a Buddha for all? In answer, the Buddha arose and went back into the world to teach others the saving truth. He went forth as the Truthfinder (the Tathagata, one who has truly arrived at Truth, *Tatha*).

The Buddha sought out five ascetics who had abandoned him earlier. During the sermon in the Deer Park at Benares (now Sarnath), the thirty-five-year-old Buddha proclaimed good news to his reluctant hearers.

---

1. Accounts differ. But all of them depict Satan doing everything in his power to dissuade Gautama. For one account see "The Assault and Temptation," http://www.ancientindia.co.uk /buddha/explore/pil2_b2.html, and "Buddha and Mara," http://mesosyn.com/myth2-1.html.

There are two extremes anyone who has given up the world must avoid: (1) a life given to pleasure, and (2) a life given to ascetic mortification. The Buddha had gained knowledge of the middle way. That way leads to insight, which leads to wisdom, which occasions calm, then on to knowledge, then to enlightenment, and finally to nirvana. Gautama appealed to the four monks to recognize him as an *arahat*, a monk who has achieved enlightenment. Once converted, the five ascetics became the sangha, the Buddhist monastic order.

# The Buddhist Order

More conversions followed until there were sixty disciples during the Buddha's itinerant ministry in northern India. They continued to multiply. Caste ceased to apply to those who joined the Buddhist order. Soon it became expedient to institute a program and compose rules for conduct. In a few years there arose a great order—the sangha. Rules for the order were simple: wear a yellow robe, adopt the shaven head, carry a begging bowl, practice daily meditation, and embrace the initiate's confession: "I take refuge in the Buddha; I take refuge in the dharma (the Truth); and I take refuge in the sangha (the order)."

Members of the sangha resolved to obey ten precepts (eventually women were admitted). The first five are lay members only:

- Refrain from destroying life (the principle of ahimsa).
- Do not take what is not given.
- Abstain from sexual activity.
- Do not lie or deceive.
- Abstain from intoxicants.
- Eat moderately and not after noon.
- Do not look on at dancing, singing, or dramatic spectacles.
- Do not show regard for garlands, scents, unguents, or ornaments.
- Do not use high or broad beds.
- Do not accept gold or silver.

For forty-five years the Buddha continued his work. In his eightieth year, he ate his noon meal. Something in the meal provoked an attack of illness. Though ill, he tried to travel, but had to lie down where he died between two sal trees.

# The Buddha's Teachings

## Philosophy

The Buddha rejected philosophical speculation as a path to enlightenment. He was too practical and plainspoken for that.

Religious devotion as a way to salvation was also rejected. All gods are finite. They are subject to death and rebirth. How could they help anyone? For salvation, one should rely upon oneself.

## The Law of Karma and Rebirth

Buddha retained, but modified, two major Hindu doctrines: (1) the Law of Karma and (2) rebirth.

He gave more flexibility to the Law of Karma than did Hindus. Anyone could undergo such a positive change of heart as to escape the full effect of sins committed in previous existences. The Law of Karma was unrelenting for anyone who continued to live by unchecked desire. But it could not bind anyone who has achieved arahatship, "the state of him that is worthy." Old karma is exhausted for anyone freed from evil desires. Once freed from "the will to live and to possess," a person's old karma is extinguished; no new karma forms.

Buddha denied the real existence of "soul" or "ego." No "soul" passes from one existence to the next. The components (skandhas) of "ego" are impermanent; they disperse at death. However, there does pass from one existence to another a "karma-laden character." Think of a seal pressed upon wax. What passes from the seal to the wax? Only the character of the seal. Just so, at death, karma-laden character—not a substantial ego—passes to a new existence in another womb.

Just as there is no permanent ego, neither is there an ultimate impersonal unity of being as the Brahmins taught. Permanence of the world and the ego is an illusion. However, karma-laden character is permanent until extinguished through enlightenment. How can this happen? Think of the flame of a candle being blown out. It is no more.

The mass of suffering in the world originates from a twelve-link cause of origination, extending from ignorance of the world's and the self's impermanence, through desire, and ending in rebirths and despair.

All composite beings, able to reason, suffer from three great flaws: (1) impermanence or anicca; (2) unreality of the self or atman (anatta); and (3) following remorsefully from the first two: sorrow (*dukkha*). Plagued by misery, people long for peace through cessation of desire. It is foolish to thirst for and cling to what is illusory. If this misery-causing thirst can be made to die, peace will follow.

How then should one live so as to obtain the joy of liberation, the termination of pain-causing desire? The answer is found in the Four Noble Truths: (1) the truth of suffering (*dukkha*, this world is incapable of satisfying), (2) the truth of the cause of suffering (*samudaya*, greed or desire), (3) the truth of the end of suffering (*nirhodha*), and (4) the truth that leads to the cessation of suffering (*magga*).

The fourth noble truth is the holy Eightfold Path: (1) right belief (in the Four Noble Truths), (2) right aspiration (having the right kind of love and avoiding all sensuality), (3) right speech, (4) right conduct (love all creatures with the right kind of love), (5) right means of livelihood, (6) right effort, (7) right mindfulness (well-disciplined thought), and (8) right meditation (the climax when all karma is consumed). The Buddha's system balances between negation and positive principles. The latter involve living so as to attain liberating desires that produce true joy. Each step is designed to lead to arahatship and finally to nirvana.

An arahat is someone who has reached the end of the Eightfold Path, "one who has awakened," one who has reached "fulfillment." He has attained wisdom and has had a foretaste of nirvana (the "blowing out" of existence) while in the trance of his enlightenment. The arahat is a Buddhist saint.

Nirvana signals termination of transmigration. The skandhas (five impermanent components or aggregates of the self)[2] having been dispersed, no "ego" and no karma remain. Does this mean "annihilation"? The Buddha would not answer this question. All he knew was that nirvana is the end of painful becoming, an eternal state of neither being nor nonbeing.

---

2. There are five skandhas: (1) the body; (2) perception; (3) feelings; (4) *samkharas* (predispositions); and (5) reason. The skandhas temporally aggregate to form a person. But upon death they disperse, leaving no ego in their wake.

To this point, no hopeful appeal to deities has been heard. There have been no supporting supernatural beings ready to help people achieve arahatship. Worship and prayer would have been absurd.

## The Religious Development of Buddhism

After the Buddha's death, things changed dramatically. For many, though not all, Buddhism developed religiously. Many followers made the Buddha the founder of a great religion, and they discovered a great company of supporting supernatural beings. Many followers took refuge *in* the Buddha instead of *in* his teaching.

In time, Buddhism became so diverse it should now be identified as a family of religions with striking similarities. Two major changes occurred. There arose a sharp division between more conservative Theravada (Hinayana, the "doctrine of the elders") Buddhism known as "little raft," and Mahayana Buddhism known as "big raft" Buddhism.

Theravada is prominent in Sri Lanka, Cambodia, Thailand, Laos, and Burma (Myanmar). Consequently, it is sometimes referred to as Southern Buddhism. Theravada Buddhism is called "little raft" because it can "carry" to nirvana only those willing to live as the Buddha taught. There is no atman (self), the world is illusory—the scene of sorrow—and nirvana is the goal. For Theravadists, the Buddha was a man, not a supernatural being. The only contact we have with him is through his teachings. There is no omnipotent Creator. Persons must make their way to enlightenment without supernatural aid.

The Theravada monk continues as the central figure. Early Buddhism is the standard. Monks strive to attain arahatship, their own enlightenment. They go forth in the morning to beg, with heads shaven, and clad in yellow robes. They follow the ancient daily schedule. They believe they have remained closest to Buddha's teachings.

Mahayana is prominent in China, Mongolia, Tibet, Korea, and Japan. It is known as "big raft" because its path to nirvana is accessible to anyone who has faith and is willing to follow the Buddha's teaching. It offers "good news" to common folk who cannot walk the Eightfold Path. Mahayana offers a multitude of benevolent saviors. It claims access to the public teachings of the Buddha and to additional secret teaching he delivered to carefully chosen disciples before his death.

Because they have access to all the Buddha taught, Mahayanists consider their form of Buddhism more authentic than Theravada. Mahayanists believe the Buddha came to earth from heaven in the form of a white elephant. He entered his mother's womb and was born as Siddhartha Gautama.

Bodhisattvas ("enlightened ones") are prominent in Mahayana Buddhism. Out of compassion, after achieving enlightenment, they have chosen to postpone entrance into nirvana in order to assist those still suffering from desire and cycles of rebirth. There is a vast pantheon of Buddhas (including female deities) and compassionate bodhisattvas to whom Buddhists can appeal. There is also a multitude of heavens, hells, and diverse explanations of nirvana.

One of the best-known forms of Mahayana Buddhism is Pure Land Buddhism. It arose in the second century BC. Pure Land Buddhism offers a path to enlightenment for those who cannot achieve the discipline laid down by the Buddha. If one will trust and love the eternal Amitabha Buddha (Immeasurable Light and Life, also known as Amida or Amitāyus), god of the Pure Land, if one will recite the name and trust in Amitabha's boundless grace, and if one will establish a personal relation with Amitabha, then the person will be reborn into the Pure Land of the Western Paradise. There everything is conducive to gaining enlightenment. Amitabha possess an inexhaustible measure of merit he wishes to share with others.

# 4
# SIKHISM

◈ ◈ ◈

Sikhism combines elements of Hinduism and Islam, with new insights to form a new religion.[1] This practice is known as syncretism.

## Nanak's Life and Work

Nanak, the founder of Sikhism, was born in AD 1469 near Lahore, India, to parents of a mercantile caste. His father was a village accountant and farmer. His mother was pious and devoted to her family. As a youth, Nanak was precocious, given to meditation and religious speculation. He loved poetry. He married, had two children, and spent his evenings singing hymns to the Creator. He and a Muslim friend, Mardana, became the center of a small group of religious seekers.

One day Nanak retired to a forest where he experienced a decisive religious experience. He described the encounter as a theophany—a divine manifestation. In a vision, Nanak was taken into God's presence. God's true nature was revealed to him. God said: "I am with thee. I have made thee happy, and also those who shall take thy name. Go and repeat Mine, and cause others to do likewise. Abide uncontaminated by the world. Practice the repetition of My name, charity, ablutions, worship, and med-

---

1. For an excellent entry into the spirit of the Sikhs see Valarie Kaur, *See No Stranger: A Memoir and Manifestation of Revolutionary Love* (New York: One World, 2020).

itation. I have given thee this cup of nectar, a pledge of my regard."[2] God had called Nanak to a life of prophecy; he would be God's apostle.

Nanak is said to have responded by uttering the preamble of the Japji ("recital"), a composition by Nanak, the most important Sikh scripture. It is repeated as a morning devotional rite by all Sikhs. It begins: "There is but one God whose name is True, the Creator." It concludes with an affirmation of God's eternality.[3]

There followed years of wide-ranging evangelism by Nanak with Mardana as his companion. Its purpose was the purification and reconciliation of religions. Nanak sang hymns of evangelism while Mardana played the rebec—a small, stringed instrument. In spite of opposition, Nanak believed his evangelism would bear fruit among his few converts. The True Name would cause the seed of the good news to increase.

When Nanak and Mardana reached the Punjab, they achieved significant success. Groups of Sikhs (disciples) began to form.

At Kartarpur, Punjab (said to be founded by Nanak), Mardana became ill and died. Nanak, now sixty-nine, died soon thereafter (1539). But before Nanak died, he appointed a successor, a disciple named Angad. Sikhs, Hindus, and Muslims gathered to mourn.

# Nanak's Teachings

Guru ("spiritual teacher") Nanak combined teachings of Hinduism and Islam. His doctrine is surprisingly simple. Its defining theme is the oneness and sovereignty of God the Creator. Monotheism is at the Sikh center. The one God is eternally one, sovereign and omnipotent. God is transcendent and immanent, both creator and destroyer. God's mercy is inexhaustible, and his love is greater than his justice. God created the world by his primal utterance (his word, logos). The world is real, but not ultimately so; that attribution belongs to God alone. God predestines everyone and all creatures. He ordains that humans, the highest creatures, be served by lower creatures.

---

2. Noss, *Man's Religions*, 223.
3. Ibid.

Nanak called God the True Name because he did not want to confuse God with names such as Allah, Rama, Shiva, or Ganesha. The True Name, the true God, is manifested in many places and is known by many names. If anyone insists on naming God, let it be *Hari*, the Kindly.

Nanak retained the Hindu doctrine of maya (the world as illusion), but not as pure illusion. Material objects, though real, can become so attractive, so powerful they "build a wall of falsehood" that separates them from the true God. Material things, though created by God, form a veil that only spiritual insight can penetrate.[4]

From Hinduism, Nanak retained samsara, the transmigration of souls. He also retained its corollary, the Law of Karma. He warned against living apart from God by succumbing to egoism and sensuous desire. Ruin results from empty ritual, whether Muslim or Hindu. Going through forms of worship without really concentrating on the divine name is a fatal distraction. The goal of the religious life is absorption into God where there is uninterrupted bliss (nirvana). Salvation does not mean going to paradise, but abolition of individuality through absorption into the True Name. Salvation awaits those who think only of God and endlessly repeat his name.

Sikhs are optimistic about redeeming the world. True religion, they believe, has a profound social mission: to improve the well-being of persons in all classes and cultures. Don't run away from the world. Do not ignore the social principles of the Qur'an. Nanak urged, "Let compassion be thy mosque, let faith be thy prayer, let honest living be thy Koran, . . . Let piety be the fasts thou keepest . . . let submission to the Lord's Will be thy rosary."[5]

Sikh congregations are called sangats. Their place of assembly is called a gurdwara ("door to the guru"). They also establish langars—community kitchens—that serve free common meals. Regardless of caste, and to promote democracy and harmony, Guru Nanak's early disciples sat together on the ground while eating.

John Noss summarizes Sikh piety:

---

4. Ibid., 224.
5. Ibid., 225.

The good man and the good Sikh is pure in motive and in act. Prefers the virtuous, seeks brotherhood with high and low without regard to caste, craves the guru's word and all divine knowledge as a man craves food, loves his wife and renounces all other women, avoids quarrelsome topics, is not arrogant, does not trample on others, and forsakes evil company, associating instead only with the holy.[6]

Nine gurus as official heads of the Sikhs succeeded Guru Nanak. Even though Guru Nanak and his followers taught peace and conciliation, persecution by the Muslim Mughal dynasty (early sixteenth to the mid-eighteenth century) forced Sikhs to arm and defend themselves. The tenth guru, Gobind Singh, Gobind the Lion (1666—1708), amid fierce opposition, exhorted Sikhs to stand firm in the faith. Not animated by enmity toward anyone, Gobind Singh urged Sikhs fearlessly to defend the truth. He created and baptized selected men into the Khalsa ("the Pure"). Those who first joined the Khalsa, and those who joined thereafter, bore the name Singh (Lion).

## Sikh Scriptures

The main scripture is the Adi Granth ("first scripture"). It is commonly called the Guru Granth Sahib. It holds the central place in gurdwaras, Sikh temples. Sikhs do not think of the Adi Granth as a holy book, but as their current and continuing eternal "guru," their guide or master. It is ritually opened each morning, wrapped up and put away at night. *Sukhasan* is the ceremony in which the Granth is put to bed.

The Adi Granth, Granth, or Granth Sahib was compiled by the fifth guru, Guru Arjun (1581-1606), to keep the Sikhs' devotional hymns from being lost. Later gurus added hymns. All copies of the Adi Granth are identical since Sikhs are forbidden to make changes.

A second Granth is the Dasam Granth ("Tenth Book"). Largely attributed to Guru Gobind Singh, the tenth guru, the Dasam Granth is a collection of hymns, philosophical writings, mythology, autobiography, and erotic fables. The Adi Granth is by far the more important of the two scriptures.

---

6. Ibid.

# 5

# JUDAISM

◈ ◈ ◈

In Judaism we meet the people of the covenant, an agreement made between the one true God (YAHWEH) and a people of God's own making, whose reason for being was in all ways to bear faithful witness to the covenant-making God. They were to do this as their *way of being and doing* (Torah, law, guidance, instruction)[1] and as a "light to the nations" (Isa. 42:6; 49:6).

We also meet a people who affirm God to be the Creator, who when creating the world called it "good" (Gen. 1:1-31) and thereby fixed Judaism's definitive disposition toward the world. Expressive of Judaism is the psalmist's exclamation: "The heavens are telling the glory of God, and the firmament proclaims his handiwork" (Ps. 19:1). The second half of the psalm (vv. 7-14) celebrates Torah, which "reviv[es] the soul" and transforms those who are simple into those who are wise (v. 7).

---

1. Ancient Israel's neighbors "served" their gods by caring for them in various ways, e.g., feeding, bathing, and bedding their images. YAHWEH did not need to be "cared" for. Israel served YAHWEH by obeying Torah, "which showed them how to love the Lord their God with all their hearts and minds and strength and be holy as Yahweh was holy." Walton says what was given at Sinai should be understood as *covenant stipulations* rather than as law *per se*. John H. Walton, *Ancient Near Eastern Thought and the Old Testament* (Grand Rapids: Baker Academic, 2006), 155, 297.

Defining Judaism is a complex task, for many voices contribute. They include the Law, the Prophets, and the Writings that form the Tanakh, the Jewish Bible. In the first century of the Common Era, voices included hellenized high priests who had made peace with the Romans and Hellenistic culture, Essenes who had washed their hands of the whole temple system as corrupt, Zealots prepared to take the sword and dispense with the hated Romans, and Pharisees, zealous for the written and oral law. There was also the great Alexandrian Jewish philosopher Philo (c. 20 BC—AD 50), who sought to integrate Judaism and Greek philosophy. All of these and many more since then contribute.

Martin Buber (1878—1965), probably the most influential twentieth-century Jewish scholar, articulated the "spirit of Judaism" in *On Judaism*. Identify Judaism not first as a religion but as a religiosity. Religion is a collection of dogmas and prescriptions handed down. Religiosity is a "longing to establish a living communion with the unconditioned." It "is an outpouring of the Holy Spirit into the person who purifies and sanctifies himself."[2] The defining character of Judaism is *holiness*, "true community with God and true community with human beings." Holiness involves the union of "the religious and the ethical," for in "genuine Judaism ethics and faith are not separate spheres." Holiness means "realizing the divine truth in the fullness of everyday life."[3] Judaism's longing for God is the desire to prepare a place for him, the true community. Its wait for the Messiah is the wait for true community.[4]

Nearly Buber's equal was Abraham Joshua Heschel (1907-72). In his classic *God in Search of Man*, every page breathes the spirit of the prophets. Heschel says Judaism is defined by "unique events that happened at particular moments in history. There are no substitutes for revelation."[5] "Israel is a spiritual order in which the human and the ultimate, the natural and the holy enter a lasting covenant, in which kinship with God is

---

2. Martin Buber, *On Judaism* (New York: Schocken Books, 1967), 80, 83.
3. Ibid., 195.
4. Ibid., 110-11.
5. Abraham Joshua Heschel, *God in Search of Man: A Philosophy of Judaism* (New York: Farrar, Straus and Giroux, 1983), 197.

not an aspiration but a reality of destiny."[6] At Sinai, Jews learned "spiritual values are not only aspirations in us but a response to a transcendent appeal addressed to us." To the discerning eye, the events of the Bible "are episodes of one great drama: the quest of God for man."[7]

# A Missionary People

According to the Tanakh the people of Israel bore the "scandal [Gr. "stumbling block"] of particularity." They were uniquely brought into existence by YAHWEH in the call to Abraham and at Sinai where the Torah was revealed through Moses. Their reason for existence was to declare God's glory, including his grace, to the nations. *That mission was their constitution.* Every revelation, deliverance, success and failure, and all hopes were to bear witness. Israel was meant to be the "called-out" congregation of the Lord by whom all life would be sanctified. Late Rabbi Jonathan Sacks, former chief rabbi of the United Hebrew Congregation of the Commonwealth, affirms this sentiment. The script of the Jewish story elicits a "breathtaking attempt to build out of simple acts and ordinary lives, a fragment of heaven on earth, a society of human dignity under the sovereignty of God, a home for the Divine presence."[8] "Every aspect of life" is to be a calibrated "choreography of holiness," a "religious drama" conducted "in terms of ordinary lives."[9] The goal of such comprehensive sanctification, echoes Rabbi Jacob Neusner, "is nothing less than the sanctification of God on high" in the everyday social order.[10]

Jewish theologian Will Herberg (1901-97) says "salvation or redemptive history" (*Heilsgeschicte*) is the "saving truth" of God's dealings with Israel, and through Israel, all humankind. Israel's history is not merely "history *for* Israel." It is "history *for* the world."[11] "Redemptive history" is

6. Ibid., 423.

7. Ibid., 197.

8. Jonathan Sacks, *A Letter in the Scroll: Understanding Our Jewish Identity and Exploring the Legacy of the World's Oldest Religion* (New York: Free Press, 2000), 221.

9. Ibid., 167.

10. Jacob Neusner, *A Rabbi Talks with Jesus*, rev. ed. (Montreal: McGill-Queen's University Press, 2000), 103.

11. Will Herberg, *Judaism and Modern Man: An Interpretation of Jewish Religion* (Woodstock, VT: Jewish Lights, 1997), 261.

"redeeming history," "history with the power to save."[12] God "plunges into human history and personally encounters" us as Redeemer.[13] To be "authentically Jewish"[14] is to make oneself "part of this redemptive history." By grace and faith, one "appropriates redemptive history as one's own."[15]

Israel was uniquely constituted to "extend YAHWEH's salvation to the ends of the earth,"[16] to become "a light to the nations" (Isa. 49:6). According to Herberg, this includes "showing forth God's greatness and graciousness as well as an active effort to bring the peoples of the world to acknowledge the Holy One of Israel." In "inward life and corporate existence and outgoing service," Israel's vocation is to "'sanctify the Name' [of YAHWEH], and to stand witness to the living God amidst the idolatries of the world."[17]

Glorious celebrations of obedience and communion included in Israel's covenants, history, temple practices (*cultus*), psalms, prophet oracles, festivals, and hopes heralded one message: "I am YAHWEH, and beside me there is no other god." He alone can rightly say, "I AM." He is and will be Lord *over* and *in* his creation. Israel's task was to live out and explain this.

## Second Temple Judaism

Israel's history of mission—its failures and successes—has many chapters.

In Jesus's day, Israel's history had arrived at what is known as Second Temple Judaism or early Judaism. The primary focus of Second Temple Judaism ranges from Alexander the Great in the late fourth century BC to the emperor Hadrian and the Bar Kokhba revolt early in the second century.

In 587/6 the Babylonians destroyed the magnificent temple built by King Solomon (Jer. 52:12-30). Israel had gone into Babylonian exile. But

12. Ibid., 287.

13. Ibid., 62.

14. Ibid., 287.

15. Ibid., 261.

16. N. T. Wright and Michael Bird, *The New Testament in Its World* (Grand Rapids: Zondervan Academic, 2019), 377.

17. Herberg, *Judaism and Modern Man*, 272. For a beautiful account of one Jewish understanding of the kingdom of God and its consummation, see chap. 18 in Herberg, *Judaism and Modern Man* (261-86).

with support from Cyrus, king of Persia—successor to the Babylonians—some Jews had returned. They rebuilt the walls of Jerusalem and the temple. They reconstituted temple worship and rigorously guarded against errors that had led to exile. Under the sponsorship of Herod the Great (74/73–c. 4 BC), the temple was extensively enriched in size and beauty (completed AD 63). It was the center of Israel's religious life.

Second Temple Judaism was supported by Four Pillars: exclusive monotheism, Torah (Pentateuch), temple, and election (Israel is God's covenant people, chosen before creation, Jub. 15:31-32; Pss. Sol. 9:8-9).

Four major sects competed to define Judaism and establish its future: the Sadducees, Pharisees, Essenes, and Zealots.

The Sadducees were in Jerusalem. They included the leading priests and other members of the urban elite. As part of the urban elite, they were bearers of the "Great Tradition," the "embodiment of the norms and values that give continuity and substance to the ideals of Israelite society."[18] They adhered to the first five books of the Bible (Pentateuch) as authoritative. They denied the resurrection of the body because it was not taught in the Pentateuch. The Sadducees cooperated with and benefitted from Rome. They vigorously defended the temple cult.

The Pharisees (Heb. *Perushim*) arose shortly after the Maccabean Revolt (167-160 BC), probably as descendants of the Hasidean ("pious ones"). Some were priests, most were not. They were fiercely loyal to the Written Torah (guidance, instruction) and held the Oral Torah (a parallel stream of revelation, given with the Written Torah) as equally binding. They insisted on compliance with the laws of purity (e.g., table fellowship and dietary laws). Not of high economic or professional standing, they were most influential in towns and villages. There were also non-elite Jerusalemite Pharisees.[19] Pharisees were predominantly opposed to Hellenistic influences.

The Essenes believed temple culture and Jewish life had so betrayed the essence of Judaism they could not be reformed. They separated from

---

18. Bruce J. Malina, *The New Testament World: Insights from Cultural Anthropology*, 3rd ed. (Louisville, KY: Westminster John Knox Press, 2001), 86.
19. Ibid., 88.

temple and public participation. They formed their own communities and awaited the coming of two Messiahs: the true anointed priest and the true Davidic king. One would preside over a renewed temple. The other would lead the Essenes—the faithful Sons of Light—in successful holy war against the Sons of Darkness. The true Israel would then rule in peace and righteousness forever.

Qumran, located on the northwestern Dead Sea shore, south of Jericho, is the best-known Essene settlement. The Dead Sea Scrolls found at Qumran are associated with the Qumran Essenes.

The Zealots (the Fourth Philosophy), founded by Judas the Galilean, were fiercely opposed to Rome. They leaned toward armed revolt. Jewish historian Flavius Josephus (AD 37-100) says Zealots "have an inviolable attachment to liberty, and say that God is to be their only Ruler and Lord. They also do not value dying any kinds of death, nor indeed do they heed the deaths of their relations and friends, nor can any such fear make them call any man lord."[20]

Since returning from exile, with the exception of rule by Jews known as the Hasmoneans, Israel had been under the control of the Persians, then the Greeks, and finally the Romans. Numerous minor revolts were quickly extinguished. But after the death of Herod Agrippa I, grandson of Herod the Great, who ruled Palestine for the Romans from AD 41 to 44, disorder increased as one Roman governor (procurator) succeeded another.

In AD 66 a fierce war between Jews and Romans erupted. Eleazar, captain of the temple and son of the high priest, convinced a group of rogue priests to cease praying for, and offering daily sacrifices on behalf of, the emperor. This open defiance marked the beginning of the war.

Roman forces were led first by Vespasian and then Titus. The struggle, conducted while Jews fought among themselves, was immensely savage. Strong resistance only accelerated Roman desire for revenge. The Romans were finally victorious in AD 70. The temple was destroyed, and many Jews were executed. Josephus details the slaughter. He says the Romans

---

20. Flavius Josephus, *Antiquities of the Jews*, bk. 18, chap. 1.6. Early Jewish Writings. http://www.earlyjewishwritings.com/text/josephus/ant18.html.

made Jerusalem "run down with blood."[21] With the city depleted, Titus left for Rome, ladened with plunder and captives.

More than the temple and city were destroyed. The priesthood and the entire sacrificial system vanished in the flames. The bond between temple and synagogue ended. An immense dispersion of Jews began. The powerful Sadducees disappeared. The Zealots, Essenes, and Herodians (supporters of the Herodian dynasty, c. 55 BC–c. AD 93) were soon to follow. The Great Sanhedrin (the supreme Jewish court system in Jerusalem)[22] lingered until the end of the Bar Kokhba revolt (AD 132-135).

A variety of reactions emerged. Brokenhearted anguish is evident in 4 Ezra and 2 Baruch. Rabbi Johanan ben-Zakkai taught that God desires deeds of loving-kindness rather than temple sacrifice. Others fanned fires of rebellion in hopes of reversing the catastrophe and constructing the true temple. After AD 135 the Pharisees came to dominate the Jewish world as rabbinic Judaism. The challenge for all was how to reestablish an authentically Jewish way of life in the absence of temple and priesthood.

Unwilling to believe all was lost, some Zealots continued to harass the Romans from the hills. The Jewish defenders of Masada (Herod's mountaintop fortress) fought on, and then committed suicide (all eight hundred) once all hope was lost (AD 74).

Amazingly, in AD 132 a final bloody revolt erupted under the leadership of a messianic aspirant named Bar Kokhba ("Son of the Star" [see Num. 24:17]). He intended to rebuild the temple and establish himself as king. The Bar Kokhba revolt was sparked in part by Emperor Hadrian condemning circumcision as a barbaric practice. Bar Kokhba and his forces captured Jerusalem and other Palestinian cities.[23]

Emperor Hadrian's response was overwhelming. Slowly, in spite of fierce resistance, the Romans took Jerusalem and much of the country-

---

21. Flavius Josephus, *War of the Jews*, bk. 6, chap. 8.5. Early Jewish Writings. http://www .earlyjewishwritings.com/text/josephus/war6.html.

22. The Great Sanhedrin was the supreme religious body. There were also smaller Sanhedrins in towns.

23. For a detailed account see "Ancient Jewish History: The Bar Kokhba Revolt (132-135 CE)," Jewish Virtual Library. https://www.jewishvirtuallibrary.org/the-bar-kokhba-revolt -132-135-ce.

side. Bethar, the rebel stronghold, fell to the Romans in AD 135. Men, women, and children were slaughtered. Hadrian then ordered Jerusalem plowed with a yoke of oxen. Many Jews were sold into slavery. The rest were forbidden to live in Jerusalem. Hadrian converted Jerusalem to a pagan city named Aelia Capitolina and erected a temple to Jupiter on the original temple site (St. Helena, mother of Constantine the Great, destroyed the Jupiter temple c. 325). Jews in Palestine were forbidden to study the Torah, observe the Sabbath, or practice circumcision.

Rabbi Akiva (c. AD 50-135), a prodigiously learned scholar, considered one of the greatest rabbinic sages, believed Bar Kokhba was the Messiah. A symbol of Jewish martyrdom, Akiva was put to death by the Romans because he insisted on teaching the Torah in public. Now that there was no temple and no high priest to make atonement for sin, Rabbi Akiva taught that sinners could obtain forgiveness simply by confessing their sins, expressing remorse, and resolving not to repeat the sin. No mediator is needed; the old system no longer exists; forgiveness now resides in a direct relationship between the individual and God.

# Making the Talmud: Central Text of Rabbinic Judaism

Judaism not only survived but thrived. After tragedy, says Jonathan Sacks, "the Jewish people made some of its greatest spiritual advances."[24] Without temple or land, in other lands and often under immense persecution, its inextinguishable religious and cultural cohesion continued.

In AD 69 Rabbi Johanan ben-Zakkai, follower of the great Rabbi Hillel (d. c. AD 10), moved to Javneh (Jamnia), a town on the coast (near modern Tel Aviv).[25] There he established an academy and set about systematizing the laws and doctrines of Judaism. As Jews had done for cen-

24. Sacks, *A Letter in the Scroll*, 141.

25. Ibid. According to the Babylonian Talmud, during the siege of Jerusalem, Rabbi ben-Zakkai was smuggled out of Jerusalem in a coffin for consultation with Roman General Vespasian, soon to become emperor. He supposedly asked Vespasian to spare the city of Javneh as a home for scholars. "To defend a country," Rabbi Sacks explains, "you need an army. But to defend an identity, you need a school. Judaism was about to become again a religion of the book, not of the sword," 163.

turies, he adapted Jewish teaching to fit the changed situation. He and his associates set lunar calendar dates for festivals.

The Javneh academy decided the organization and contents of the Hebrew Bible, the Tanakh. The recognized books were organized into three parts: Torah (Law, the Pentateuch), Nebiim (Prophets), and Kethubim (Writings).[26]

The most important product of Jewish scholars after the destruction of Jerusalem in AD 70 was the Talmud ("study" or "teaching"). The Talmud is composed of two parts: the Mishnah and the Gemara (or Gemorah).

## The Mishnah

In addition to providing a detailed study of Written Torah, the Javneh academy worked to define the oral law. Interpretations and opinions (Midrash) of the oral law had through the centuries been conveyed by learned rabbis. All rules and judgments had to be sorted out and explained. The result is the Mishnah ("review" or "repetitions") produced in Palestine c. AD 200 by Rabbi Judah the Prince (or Patriarch, c. AD 135-c. 220), descendant of Rabbi Hillel. Earlier work by Rabbi Akiva (c. AD 50-135) and by Rabbi Meir (mid-second century) provided the basis for the Mishnah. It is the first major written collection of the Oral Torah. It is also the first major work of rabbinic literature.

Rabbi Judah arranged the oral law under six orders: sedarim agriculture, festivals, marriage, civil law, the temple service, and ritual purity. Later they were rearranged under fourteen headings by the great Medieval Jewish scholar and physician Moses Maimonides (1135-1204). The fourteen headings are: The Book of Knowledge, The Book of Love [of God], The Book of Seasons, The Book of Women, The Book of Holiness, The Book of Utterances, The Book of Seeds, The Book of Temple Service, The Book of Sacrifices, The Book of Purity, The Book of Damages, The Book of Acquisition, The Book of Civil Laws, and The Book of Judges.

---

26. The Tanakh, Jewish Virtual Library. https://www.jewishvirtuallibrary.org/the-tanakh -full-text.

John B. Noss observes: one reads the Mishnah "with a sense of wonder at its microscopic examination of every phase of Jewish life." It "fed the soul" of Judaism.[27]

Oral tradition that did not make it into the Mishnah was collected in a separate volume known as the Tosefta (appendix, or supplement).

## The Gemara ("supplementary learning," "completion")

Scholars in Palestine (Israel) and Babylonia (modern Iraq) subsequently commented on the Mishnah.[28] They worked out its inner logic and showed how its teachings are based upon the Hebrew Scriptures. They also showed connections between the Mishnah and the Tosefta. At first the Gemara was transmitted orally only; writing it was forbidden. That changed when Rabbi Judah the Prince published the Gemara around AD 200. Previously unrecorded halakah ("the path one walks," religious laws derived from the Written and Oral Torah) and haggadah (aggadah, non-legalistic exegetical texts) were combined to form the Gemara.

Palestinian and Babylonian sages developed their own Gemaras. The result was two Talmuds: the Jerusalem Talmud (*Talmud Yerushalmi*, completed c. 350) and the Babylonian Talmud (*Talmud Bavli*, completed c. 500, further edited for another two centuries). The latter is the most influential.

Today the Talmud provides the framework for the various forms of Judaism.

# The Kabbalah

During the Middle Ages, a form of Judaism arose that continues to flourish. It is known as kabbalism. The kabbalists believed they had access to the secret meanings of the Hebrew Scriptures. They engaged in speculative theology and developed a mystical number system that gave access to the Hebrew Bible's deeper meaning. They discerned mysterious arrangements of words and numbers that surface study misses. Their sys-

---

27. Noss, *Man's Religions*, 399-400.
28. A distinction is made between the tannaim ("rehearsers"), teachers who flourished in Palestine in the first two centuries; and the amoraim ("expounders"), teachers who flourished in both Palestine and Babylon from the third to the end of the fifth century.

tem of numbers, based upon the Hebrew alphabet, permitted them to learn God's various names and attributes. Their most important written authority is a group of books named the Zohar ("radiance"). It was developed in the 1280s by Moses de Leon of Spain who attributed the work to a second-century rabbi. The Zohar "contains a mystical discussion of the nature of God, the origin and structure of the universe, the nature of souls, sin, redemption, and good and evil."[29] The kabbalists also wrestled with the question of how a perfect God could produce an imperfect or incomplete world.[30]

## Contemporary Forms of Judaism

The complexity of contemporary Judaism cannot be addressed. Here only major branches are identified.

### Orthodox Judaism

Orthodox Judaism is a collective term. There are distinctions (e.g., the ultra-Orthodox, or Haredi). Orthodox Jews advocate strict observance of Jewish law in accordance with unbroken instruction received through the ages. Orthodox Jews believe God elected the Jews and bound that election with a covenant. They regard both the Written and Oral Torah as divinely revealed to Moses on Mount Sinai and faithfully transmitted since then. Orthodox Jews obey prescribed dietary, purity, and ethical laws by which God becomes and remains present in everyday Jewish life. Most anticipate arrival of the Messiah (Mashiach, "the anointed one"), a great judge and political leader, Son of David. He will rebuild the Jerusalem temple and govern the world in righteousness.[31]

29. "Kabbalah: The Zohar," Jewish Virtual Library. https://www.jewishvirtuallibrary.org/the-zohar. "The Zohar," The Kabbalah Centre, February 8, 2013. https://kabbalah.com/en/master-kabbalists/the-zohar.

30. For a discussion of kabbalism see "Kabbalah and Jewish Mysticism," Judaism 101. http://www.jewfaq.org/kabbalah.htm.

31. The anticipated Messiah will be human, not divine-human as in Christianity. Neither will he be a savior as Christians believe Jesus to be. For a recent example of messianic expectation by Orthodox rabbis see Ryan Jones, "Top Rabbis: Look at the Signs, Messiah Is Coming!", *Israel Today*, August 3, 2020. https://www.israeltoday.co.il/read/top-rabbis-look-at-the-signs-messiah-is-coming/. See also "Mashiach: The Messiah," Judaism 101. https://www.jewfaq.org/mashiach.htm.

The Hasidic movement (Hasidism), founded in Eastern Europe in the 1700s, is a prominent part of Orthodox Judaism. Its founder was Rabbi Israel Baal Shem Tov (referred to as the "Besht"). There are at least a dozen branches of Hasidism devoted to the revealed inner (mystical) and outer aspects of the Torah. Unlike more intellectual forms of Judaism, without diminishing the importance of Torah study, the Hasidim ("those who keep faith with the covenant") value a way of Jewish life that emphasizes the ability of all Jews to grow closer to God through everything they do, say, and think. They emphasize constant focus on attachment to God.[32] The Hasidim are quite influential in Judaism, especially in Israel and New York City. The best-known twentieth-century representative of Hasidism was Martin Buber, author of the philosophical masterpiece *I And Thou* (1923). Buber says, "The core of Hasidic teachings is the concept of a life of fervor, of exalted joy."[33]

## Reform (or Progressive) Judaism

Reform Judaism arose in response to the modern period of European history when Jews were permitted to leave their ghettos and "assimilate" into European culture. Its primary mover was the German philosopher Moses Mendelssohn (1729-86). Reform Judaism cast off much of Orthodox belief and practice. It attempted to adapt Judaism to modern changes in social, political, and cultural life. It provided a way for Jews to accept innovation while preserving tradition. A Reform Jew is permitted to decide whether or not to embrace a particular traditional Jewish belief or practice. Reason, formal education, participation in the public order, and individual autonomy are vital.

As a sign of changes in Israel, on March 23, 2021, Rabbi Gilad Kariv, president and CEO of the Israel Movement for Reform and Progressive Judaism, became the first Reform rabbi to be elected to Israel's Knesset.[34]

---

32. See "Orthodox Judaism: Hassidism," Jewish Virtual Library. https://www.jewishvirtuallibrary.org/hasidism.
33. Martin Buber, *Tales of the Hasidim: The Early Masters* (New York: Schocken Books, 1970), 2.
34. Jeffrey Salkin, "The Day Reform Judaism Made History," Religion News Service, March 24, 2021. https://religionnews.com/2021/03/24/israel-elections-reform-rabbi-gil-kariv/.

## Conservative Judaism

Conservative Judaism arose as a reaction against Reform Judaism. Conservative Jews believe Reform Judaism went too far in its efforts to accommodate modernity by modifying Jewish belief and practice. Conservative Jews seek to preserve Jewish tradition and ritual, while treating both with more flexibility than Orthodox Jews permit. Contemporary conditions must be taken into account when deciding how to be a faithful Jew.

Currently there is serious discussion regarding the possibility of Reform and Conservative Judaism merging. Differences between the two have narrowed to the extent that many question their continued separation.[35]

## Reconstructionist Judaism

Reconstructionist Judaism (also known as Reconstructing Judaism[36]) emerged in the twentieth century under the leadership of Mordecai Kaplan. According to Reconstructionism, Judaism is not a religion fixed by Scripture and revelation. Rather, it is the evolving civilization of the Jewish people. Guided by historical memory, Judaism rightly changes over time. Traditional "divine commandments" are not binding. Judaism includes Jewish culture and philosophy. Jewish rituals are "folkways." There are about one hundred Reconstructionist synagogues in the United Stated and elsewhere.

In 1926 the World Union for Progressive Judaism was established and headquartered in Jerusalem. The WUPJ is the international network of the Reform, Liberal, Progressive, and Reconstructionist movements. It serves 1,200 congregations with 1.8 million members in more than fifty countries.

---

35. Jeffrey Salkin discusses the advisability of merger between the two branches of Judaism in "Should Reform and Conservative Judaism Merge?" He says, "Non-Orthodox rabbis (and some modern Orthodox rabbis as well) increasingly share worldviews on matters of ritual, social justice, etc." (Religion News Service, May 19, 2020). https://religionnews.com/2020/05/19/reform-conservative-merger/.

36. Reconstructing Judaism (Home). https://www.reconstructingjudaism.org/.

# 6

# ISLAM

❖ ❖ ❖

Islam is a vibrant, worldwide religion numbering approximately 1.8 billion communicants. It accounts for nearly one-fourth of the world's population.[1]

## The Prophet Muhammad

Muhammad ("highly praised," c. 571-632), founder of Islam, was born in Mecca, Arabia (modern Saudi Arabia). The Quraysh, the tribe into which Muhammad was born, venerated a distant high god named Allah.

Most Arabs worshipped local gods and goddesses, including astral deities. Some were strictly local. Others presided over certain geographical regions. In Mecca, a mother-goddess, the goddess of fate, and al-'Uzza, the morning star, were worshipped. Many idols were venerated.

Orphaned by age six, Muhammad was reared first by his grandfather and later by his uncle Abu Talib. Known in his youth as al-Amin ("the trustworthy"), Muhammad grew up in poverty. As a youth he shared the religious beliefs of his community. This included worship of Hubal and al-'Uzza, belief in jinn (fire-created spirits that could appear to humans or remain invisible), angels, Satan, and omens regarding the future.

---

1. "Muslims and Islam," Pew Research Center. https://www.pewresearch.org/fact-tank/2017/08/09/muslims-and-islam-key-findings-in-the-u-s-and-around-the-world/

As he matured, Muhammad became increasingly disturbed by the religious beliefs and practices of his people. He was dissatisfied with tribal quarreling, drinking, gambling, and the ever-present polytheism. He became receptive to belief in one God, the last judgment, and living righteously. In addition to Muhammad's own reflective spirit, growth of his beliefs seems to have come from various sources. These included Christians and Jews who, passing through Mecca in commercial caravans, expounded their faiths during commercial fairs.

Muhammad was hired by a wealthy Qurayshite widow named Khadija to serve in her trading caravans. She was so impressed by Muhammad's honesty and diligence that, though fifteen years his senior, in 595 she became his wife. She loved and mothered him and encouraged his religious quests.

## Religious Awakening

Muhammad's religious search entered a period of crisis. He had been deeply impressed by belief in a final judgment shared by Jews and Christians. A time was approaching when the One God would punish idolatry and other sins in everlasting fire. Muhammad was agitated by fear that God's judgment would fall upon his own people. Only inspired prophets, not vain idols, could speak for the one true God. He had sent prophets to people in Palestine and Persia. Would not God send a prophet to Arabia?

Waraqah, a cousin of Khadija and companion of Muhammad, provided encouragement for Muhammad's search (Waraqah may have been a Christian). So did Zaid, a Christian slave boy whom Muhammad had adopted.

With the last judgment near, Muhammad, now about forty years old, went into the hills above Mecca to brood privately.

## Muhammad's Prophetic Call

For days Muhammad visited a cave near Mount Hira. Suddenly one night in the year AD 610, "the Night of Power and Excellence," the angel Gabriel appeared. Gabriel cried out, "Recite: In the Name of thy Lord."

According to Sura 96 of the Qur'an, when the vision ended, Muhammad reproduced the entire revelation. Sura 53 defends the authenticity of the revelation. Half doubting and half believing, fearing for his sanity, Muhammad rushed home to share news with Khadija.

After many months of self-questioning, Muhammad came to see himself as a true prophet (nabi) and apostle (*rasul*) of Allah. The revelations continued. At last Allah had given a prophet to Arabia, and a scripture of greater authority than those of Jews and Christians.

## The First Meccan Ministry

"In the name of the Lord," Muhammad began to recite the revelations he had received. He preached in the streets and the courtyard of the Ka'ba.[2] His listeners ridiculed him, in part because he claimed to be a prophet. Undaunted, day after day he returned and warned of impending judgment and called people to repent. He also emphasized social justice and service to the poor.

Muhammad's first Meccan ministry continued with only marginal success. Persecution intensified. Muhammad was forced from public places. After ten years, Muhammad's converts numbered about forty.

Facing persistent opposition, Muhammad began seeking another way to fulfill his calling. After consultations with men from Yathrib, a city three hundred miles to the north, Muhammad was invited to take charge of the city. Blood feuds between rival clans had caused civil disorder. Perhaps Muhammad could resolve the unrest.

## The Hijra (departure or flight)

In AD 622 Muhammad and his kinsman Abu Bakr, who later became Muhammad's successor, fled from Mecca to Yathrib. Their departure was known as the Hijra.

## The Yathrib Theocracy

After several years of successful leadership in Yathrib, Muhammad gained almost complete control. There he established the first mosque. A form of religious life was developed that would uniformly characterize Islam. It included weekly services on Friday, a call to prayer from the mosque's

---

2. The Ka'ba was a pre-Islamic shrine, believed to have been constructed by Abraham and Ishmael. It housed a sacred black stone sent from heaven.

roof (at first only on Friday, and later daily at appointed times), prostration during prayer, and receiving alms for the poor and mosque support.

In Muhammad's honor the city's name was changed to Medina (City of the Prophet). From there Muhammad and armed supporters attacked a Meccan caravan. War with Mecca resulted. The Meccans tried unsuccessfully to conquer Medina; a defensive ditch had been dug around the city. Finally, in January 630 Muhammad and ten thousand armed men attacked Mecca. The city surrendered and Muhammad took control. With the exception of a few Meccan residents, Muhammad declared a general amnesty. He had become the greatest chief in Arabia.

One of Muhammad's first acts was to go to the Ka'ba. He circled the shrine seven times before ordering the destruction of its idols. He scraped from its walls the paintings of Abraham and the angels. Nearby opponents were silenced. Distant tribes were ordered to swear allegiance to Muhammad. He was determined to achieve moral elevation and unity among the Arabs. He was on the way to creating a theocracy. Just before his sudden death in 632 Muhammad announced in a Meccan sermon a central tenet of Islam. He proclaimed "every Muslim is a brother unto every other Muslim. Ye are now one brotherhood."

Muhammad had failed to appoint a successor. Upon his death a controversy regarding leadership almost destroyed the young Muslim movement. To prevent that, his kinsman, Abu Bakr was chosen as successor (or caliph). But controversy regarding who should succeed Muhammad did not end. Should leadership rest with a family member or with some non-family candidate? To that dispute is owed the current and sometimes bitter division between Sunni (87-90%) and Shiite (or Shia, 10-13%) Muslims.

In time, divergent groups appealed to Muhammad and developed Islam in directions he probably never intended. Sunni Muslims generally view Shiites with suspicion.

## The Faith and Practice of Islam

Given the complexity of Islam, little more than an outline is offered here.

The term "muslim" is a verb that means "to accept," "to submit," "to commit oneself." A "Muslim" is "one who submits to Allah (God)" or "one who commits himself to Islam (obedience and peace)." One who declares "I am a Muslim" is doing far more than declaring membership in a religion. He is declaring, "I commit myself to Allah."

Through the centuries, Muslims have embraced one scripture, the Qur'an (or Koran, "recitation"),[3] written in Arabic. Few changes—Muslims say none—have occurred. It is believed to be the literal transcript of God's word revealed to Muhammad. Unlike other scriptures that have been altered, the Qur'an is said to be a literal copy of its heavenly archetype. The Qur'an is divided into 114 chapter-like units called suras. Except for the first, which is only seven verses, the succeeding suras are arranged mostly in decreasing length.

The second written source of guidance for Muslims, though not on the level of the Qur'an, is the hadith ("news" or "story"). It is revered as a major source of religious law and moral guidance. It records the traditions and sayings of Muhammad and his daily practices (sunna). The hadith discloses the spirit of Islam, but it is not uniformly interpreted.

The faith and practice of Islam are often treated under three headings.

## Articles of Faith (*iman*)

The *first* and most important is: "There is no God but God (Allah)." God is one; he the Creator. God is "all-seeing," "all-hearing," and "all-willing." He is transcendent, the Wholly Other One. God guides people through Muhammad, the Qur'an, and angels. Satan is a fallen angel who tries to obstruct Allah's sovereign plans.

The *second* article of faith is that "Muhammad is God's prophet (messenger)." There were many prophets before Muhammad, such as Abraham, Moses, and Jesus. But Muhammad is superior to them. He is God's final word to humankind. He completes and corrects all earlier revelations. Fully human, he is the "seal" of all prophets who came before him.

## Right Conduct (*ihsan*)

Muslims are provided comprehensive instruction for conducting themselves according to the articles of faith. John Noss comments we

---

3. The Holy Qur'an, trans. A. Yusuf Ali, https://quranyusufali.com/.

should recognize how reformatory Islam's moral instruction is.[4] Rules for right conduct include prohibitions against alcoholic drinks and gambling, regulations regarding relationships between the sexes, sharing one's substance with kinsmen, orphans, fidelity to one's parents, protection of one's children, abstention from fornication, and always acting justly.

## Religious Duty (ʻibadat)

Religious duty is summed up in the five pillars (al-arkan) of Islam.

*First*, repetition of the creed (shahada). "There is no god but Allah, and Muhammad is his prophet."

*Second*, prayer (salat). A faithful Muslim establishes five times for prayer each day. The sequence is: dawn, midday, midafternoon, sunset, and after darkness has begun (or at bedtime). During prayer, one first rolls out a prayer rug, stands reverently and offers certain prayers, bows down toward Mecca with hands on knees, offers to Allah praise and expressions of submission, stands again while praising God, falls prostrate with one's forehead on the ground (while praising God). Then one sits reverently and offers a petition. Finally, a Muslim once more prostrates himself before God. Throughout, "Allah akbar" ("God is the greatest") is repeated. It is common to pray the al-Fātiḥah (the first sura). "Praise belongs to God, the Lord of all being."

Each Friday Muslims gather as a brotherhood in mosques (usually at noon) to worship under the leadership of an imam. No class or racial distinctions are made as men gather for prayer. Shoes have been left outside. Women congregate in another section.

*Third*, almsgiving (zakat). This involves a freewill offering for the poor, slaves, strangers, beggars, and support for various charities.

*Fourth*, fasting during the month of Ramadan. Unless one is sick, or on a taxing journey, each Muslim must fast. Beginning at the break of dawn, no food or drink may be consumed until sundown. Then, only enough food can be consumed to prepare for the next day's fast.

---

4. Noss, *Man's Religions*, 310.

*Fifth*, pilgrimage (hajj). If possible, all Muslims should make a pilgrimage to Mecca at least once in their lifetime.[5] Pilgrims should be present in Mecca during the month of Dhu'l-Hijjah, the twelfth month of the Muslim lunar year. The hajj begins on the eighth day of Dhu'l-Hijjah. Nearly two million Muslims might participate each year. The hajj lasts three to five days.

Upon entering the sacred precincts of Mecca, male pilgrims must wear two lengths of white cloth without seams. They abstain from food or drink by day and do no harm to animals or vegetables. The ceremonies begin by circumambulating the Ka'ba seven times.[6] The Ka'ba, located in the Grand Mosque, is the most holy site of Islam. The lesser pilgrimage comes next. It consists of trotting, shoulders shaking, seven times between two low hills (Dafa and Marva) across the valley from each other. The lesser pilgrimage repeats Hagar's frantic attempt to find water for her son Ishmael (cf. Gen. 16:7-8). Then the greater pilgrimage begins as pilgrims move in mass toward 'Arafat, nine miles to the east. Prescribed activities are fulfilled. The final three days of the pilgrimage are spent in feasting, conversation, and merrymaking. As a final act, pilgrims return to Mecca and circle the Ka'ba once more.

After the pilgrims return home, they may be given the honorific title hajji, meaning one who has performed the hajj.

## Shariah, Jihad, and Fatwa

Three terms often misunderstood by non-Muslims are "sharia," "jihad," and "fatwa."

"Shariah" is Islamic law derived from the Qur'an and the hadith. Though authoritative, sharia is not a body of codified law in the modern sense. Instead, it is a living, decentralized, and contingent body of principles meant to guide all aspects of life. Part of what makes sharia so

---

5. For an informative video of the hajj, go to https://www.bing.com/videos/search?q=video+of+the+hajj&&view=detail&mid=5017893CDF6629EB94165017893CDF6629EB9416&&FORM=VDRVRV&ajf=60; https://www.bing.com/videos/search?q=video+of+the+hajj&&view=detail&mid=B1EEC8DA1ADCE3AD9237B1EEC8DA1ADCE3AD9237&&FORM=VDRVRV&ajf=60.

6. For a picture of the Ka'ba see https://www.learnreligions.com/steps-of-hajj-2004318.

puzzling for non-Muslims is that Muslim jurists and judges interpret it in different ways. Moreover, Muslims differ in how they observe sharia.

"Jihad" means struggle or effort. Muslims use the term to refer to various kinds of struggle: (1) the inner and outer struggle as a Muslim seeks to abide by affirmations of submission to Allah; (2) the struggle to form society in harmony with Muslim principles; (3) working to teach non-Muslims the meaning of Islam; and (4) the struggle to defend Islam, with force if necessary. Legal, diplomatic, economic, or political means should be employed first. If military force becomes necessary, there are strict rules of engagement.[7]

"Fatwa" is an Islamic legal pronouncement. It is made by an authority in religious law (mufti). A fatwa is issued to resolve a question where Islamic jurisprudence is not clear.[8]

7. "Jihad: A Misunderstood Concept from Islam," Islamic Supreme Council of America. https://wpisca.wpengine.com/?p=9.

8. "What Is a Fatwa?" The Islamic Supreme Council of America. http://wpisca.wpengine .com/?p=106.

# 7
# BRIEF SUMMARIES OF OTHER RELIGIOUS TRADITIONS

## Taoism

The founder of Taoism is believed to have been Lao Tzu (or Lao Tan). This legendary Chinese scholar is believed to have been born in the state of Ch'u (China) in 604 BC. His teachings are contained in the *Tao Te Ching*, or *Treatise of the Tao and Its Power*.

Taoism (pronounced Dowism) began as a philosophy, but for many it eventually developed religious characteristics. Its history, deities, and beliefs are complex. Unlike Judaism, Christianity, and Islam, Taoism is not a well-defined religion.

The eternal Tao is the center of Taoist philosophy. It is "the way," "the correct way to go" of the universe. It characterizes heaven and earth. Eternal, it is the source of perfection, harmony, integration, and cooperation for all things. As ultimate independent reality, it transcends all mere human preferences. First the Tao, then the universe, including all life, following its way. The Tao tends toward health, peace, and prosperity. Harm and evil result when people fail to abide by it. The Tao governed on earth during the Golden Age, a time of earthly paradise.

At its heart, as a philosophy Taoism involves humans knowing and conforming to the Tao in all thinking and living, but never attempting to control it. "The Tao that can be trodden [manipulated] is not the enduring and unchanging Tao."[1] Humans have one defining responsibility: learn the way of the Tao and fully cooperate with it. Wise persons move with the Tao. They practice *wu-wei* (quietism, no-meddlesome action), and accept the alterations of life, the interplay of the yin and the yang, two interacting energy modes.

If the Tao were ever to be carefully practiced everywhere, heaven, humankind, and earth would form a single, harmonious whole. All parts would facilitate universal well-being.[2]

The danger is that through a mixture of magic and religion, people will try to manipulate the Tao. For many, yielding to that impulse led to transforming a philosophy into a religion complete with deities, incantations, prayers, assisting priests, temples, and sects. Taoism as religion attempts to "manipulate" the Tao for such things as material well-being and immortality.

There are Taoist teachers who still teach Taoism as a philosophy instead of a religion.

As a religion, in China Taoism is dead, though many people still cling to it as magic. However, according to the 2005 Taiwan census, 33 percent of the Taiwanese populace identified as Taoist. But it is difficult to make a sharp distinction between Taoist and Buddhist adherents. As of 2015, there were 9,485 registered Taoist temples in Taiwan. There are thousands of Taoist deities. Lao Tzu, founder of Taoism, for whom manipulating the Tao was unthinkable, would be horrified by the religious development of his philosophy.

A penetrating consideration of the *Tao* from a Western and modern perspective is found in *The Abolition of Man* by C. S. Lewis. Lewis defines and defends the *Tao* against moral and value relativism and subjectivism.

---

1. *The Tao Te Ching*, I.1.1. Internet Archives. http://classics.mit.edu/Lao/taote.1.1.html.
2. Noss, *Man's Religions*, 237.

He observes, "Only those who are practicing the *Tao* will understand it."[3] Interestingly, Lewis says the Tao "admits of development from within," a development that can occur only for those firmly governed by the *Tao*.[4] To abandon the *Tao* is to enter a moral void.[5]

# Confucianism

The teachings of Confucius (c. 551-479 BC)—better known in China as Master Kong (Chinese: *Kongzi*)—and Mencius or Master Meng (c. 371-c. 289 BC), whose development of orthodox Confucianism (Chinese *Ru-jia*) earned him the title "second sage," have had an immeasurable impact upon East Asian intellectual and social history. Confucianism should be understood as a profound and comprehensive philosophy of life, not as a religion. John Noss calls it an "optimistic humanism."[6]

Little can be known with certainty about Confucius. Although scholars disagree over the origin and nature of the *Analects*, they are the main source for learning about Confucius's life and teachings. The teachings that can be confidently obtained are principally philosophical and ethical. Confucius taught that Tian (heaven) manifests the moral order of the world. It should govern all dimensions of human existence. This will require comprehensive compliance and will be achieved by carefully observing li (ritual propriety). Observance must begin with rulers, officials, and teachers who are "profound persons" (*junzi*) and continue through the family and all social relationships—through all "small persons" (*xiaoren*). The head of state should be chief exemplar of Tian. When this happens, the whole of life will be correctly ordered. Moral power (de or te) is contagious. Beginning with rulers, by obedience to the will of heaven, and careful observance of li, moral formation will spread through all aspects of life. Earth harmonized with heaven will result. Think of the wind blowing across a wheat field. All heads of grain bend to the wind's influence.

---

3. C. S. Lewis, *The Abolition of Man* (New York: Macmillan, 1947), 32.
4. Ibid., 30.
5. Ibid., 41.
6. Noss, *Man's Religions*, 265.

Mencius taught that everyone is born with an innate goodness that can be cultivated so as to comport with Tian or be squandered. But there is nothing characteristically religious about this teaching.

Confucianism has gone through numerous iterations. Between the ninth and eleventh centuries it experienced a revival known as Neo-Confucianism, inspired by philosopher Zhu Xi (1130-1200). During the Chinese Cultural Revolution of the Mao era (1966-76), Confucianism was opposed as superstitious and socially degrading. Today the Chinese Communist Party encourages Confucius's teachings because it is believed they, as interpreted by the Chinese Communist Party, will substantiate central government authority, and because its moral teachings encourage widespread restraint against individual and social corruption.

In recent years, a most intriguing development, which sinologist and political theorist Thomas A. Metzger labels "Chinese utopianism," has developed among Chinese intellectuals and beyond. For Neo-Confucianists, humanity's golden age existed in the distant past (1042-1035 BC). Since then, humanity has declined. The new moral utopianism replaces that negative assessment. Confucianism, modern Western notions of historical progress, and Marxist-Leninist utopianism have combined to form a new social philosophy. Philosopher Zhao Tingyang of Peking University is a leading proponent. He envisions a global moral revolution in which partiality will be eradicated, diplomatic tensions will become obsolete, and cultures of the world will respect one another. The concrete here and now will be made morally perfect. Politics will become an art of transforming enmity into friendship. As opposed to Western culture, Chinese culture has no concept of a fall or of restrictive original sin.[7]

## Zoroastrianism

Zoroastrianism is an ancient religion whose founder was Zarathustra, known by the Greeks as Zoroaster. He lived and taught in ancient Persia. The dates and many details of his life are uncertain. Some sources say he might have lived as early as 1750 BC. Others place him in the seventh

7. Eric Hendriks-Kim, "Why China Loves Conservatives," in *First Things*, January 2023, 23-24.

century BC. In an environment marked by polytheism (many deities), Zarathustra taught there is one supreme God and creator, Ahura Mazda, "Lord of Life and Wisdom," who expresses his will through a holy spirit and various modes of divine action. The moral law that requires human righteousness proceeds from Ahura Mazda. Humans have the freedom to obey or disobey God's will.

Though Ahura Mazda is supreme, he is not unopposed. He is contested by Angra Mainyu, the "Bad Spirit." At the world's beginning, the good spirit proceeding from Ahura Mazda was met and opposed by an evil spirit, later called Shaitin or Satan. Each person's soul is the seat of war between good and evil, the outcome of which each person must determine, either by obedience to righteousness or to evil. The influence of evil is not eternal. Zarathustra had no doubt that in the fullness of time Ahura Mazda would triumphantly overthrow all evil. There will be a general resurrection of the dead when everyone will be tested by fire—destruction for all who have chosen evil, and divine kindness for all who have chosen righteousness.

While much ancient Zoroastrian literature no longer exists, the Avesta constitutes its scripture. There are five parts: the Yasna, containing the Gathas or hymns of Zarathustra; the Visperad, festival observances; the Yashts, hymns of praise; the Vendidad, ancient purity laws; and the Khordeh Avesta, daily prayers.

Although the number of Zoroastrians is small (110,000-120,000) by comparison with major religions, Zoroastrian communities or centers exist worldwide, including throughout the United States. Most Zoroastrians live in Iran and India.

## Shinto

Shinto is the indigenous religion of Japan. The name means "the way of the kami"—sacred power of the gods. Shinto has no founder, no sacred scriptures, and no system of doctrines. But there are compilations of ancient myths and traditional teachings. Shinto is more a set of values than a formulation of religious dogma. Its central values are purity, harmony with nature, sincerity, family respect, subordination of the individual to the group, and celebration of the present.

Shinto devotees venerate invisible spiritual powers called kami (spirits) that reside in everything. Adherents seek to live in agreement with the ways of the kami. Many Japanese practice prescribed rituals (more important than doctrine) that enable them to communicate with kami. These life-giving and harmonizing powers intervene to promote human happiness when implored and treated respectfully. Kami can affect natural forces and human events. They live in Shinto shrines (*jinja*). The most important kami is the sun goddess Amaterasu. A *kannushi* (priest) mediates between worshippers and guardian deities.

Although a distinction is made between the visible and invisible world, the universe constitutes a unified reality. Humans can become kami after death.

There are three major types of Shinto.

1. Shrine Shinto (*Jinja Shinto*) is successor to State Shinto, which equated Shinto with the Japanese state. State Shinto was disbanded by Allied occupation forces at the end of WWII. Shrine Shinto focuses on worship in public shrines. There are over 80,000 Shinto shrines in Japan and many small roadside shrines. Shrine rituals, overseen by Shinto priests, are highly formalized. They include purification rites, rites of life, health, birth, weddings, and funerals.

   Each town or village has at least one shrine, residence of the local kami. Shrines are characterized by beauty and calm. One enters by way of a torii (sacred gateway).

2. Sect Shinto (*Kyoha Shinto*) developed in the 1870s. It consists of thirteen recognized sects. Although they support the broad aims of Shrine Shinto, they are more "religious" and "syncretistic" in nature. Adherents worship the kami and venerate their founders. They are usually associated with a particular shrine.

3. Folk Shinto (*Minzoku Shinto*) is not formally organized. It is the product of ordinary people. It is not systematized and does not rely upon shrine priests. Rituals can be performed by a layperson. Folk Shinto encourages a form of spirituality based on nature and ancestral spirits.

# The Bahá'í Faith

Founded in the nineteenth century, Bahá'í is one of the newest religions. It is monotheistic. Originally an offshoot of Shia Islam, Bahá'í has freely incorporated other religious sources, including Hinduism and Buddhism. Bahá'ís believe progressive revelations of God occur through manifestations to great religious leaders.[8]

In 1844 a merchant who referred to himself "the Báb" ("the Gate") began preaching in Persia (Iran). His message was deeply mystical. He believed the world was on the verge of a new and glorious era. He proclaimed a God whose essence was fundamentally unknowable. But his attributes are love, justice, mercy, and compassion. Thousands were attracted to his message.

The Báb announced God would soon send a prophet similar to Moses, Jesus, and Muhammad. He urged purity of heart as preparation for the prophet's arrival. Because the Báb rejected Muhammad as the final prophet, in 1850 in Tabriz, Iran, he was executed, along with most of his leading supporters.

One of the Báb's surviving followers became his successor. In 1852, while imprisoned in a subterranean dungeon, he received a revelation that he was the promised prophet. He called himself Bahá'u'lláh, "the glory of God." In 1863, Bahá'u'lláh announced to a small group of Bábis that he was the expected prophet. Bahá'u'lláh is the recognized founder of Bahá'í.

While under intense persecution by the Persian and Ottoman Empires, Bahá'u'lláh composed one of the key Bahá'í texts, the Kitab-i-Aqdas, and other works and letters. He also chose Haifa, Israel, as the burial site for the Báb. The impressive structure and gardens, and the Seat of the Universal House of Justice—governing body of the Bahá'ís—overlook the Mediterranean Sea. When Bahá'ís pray, they face that direction.

Bahá'ís teach the value of all religions and the equality of all persons. They stress the harmony of religion and science. They campaign for

---

8. See Bahá'í Prayers: A Selection of Prayers Revealed by Bahá'u'lláh, the Báb, and 'Abdu'l-Bahá by Bahá'u'lláh, and The Báb and 'Abdu'l-Bahá Project Gutenberg, http://www.gutenberg.org/files/19240/19240-h/19240-h.html.

social reform and international justice. The Bahá'í Faith has expanded worldwide, especially in majority world countries. It is believed to have between five to eight million adherents.

# PART II
## Why Continue to Confess Christ as Lord of All?

# 8

# A RESURRECTION FAITH OR NOTHING AT ALL

The Christian faith is a resurrection (Gr. *anastasis*) faith or nothing at all. Either God the Father confirmed the witness of Jesus of Nazareth by raising him from the dead on Easter morning, or he did not.

New Testament scholar Paul Meyer states bluntly: "On the level of sober historical reality Jesus' career had ended in failure, his teaching and above all the expectations he had generated in his followers were finally discredited by the deliberately demeaning way in which the end of his life was taken from him."[1] It appeared to be nothing but meaningless horror.

If Jesus had been an imposter, God would have settled the question by letting his body decompose, as other corpses do. In a secondary burial, his bones might have been placed in an ossuary (small stone chest) after the flesh decayed. And Jesus of Nazareth might have become a footnote somewhere in Jewish history, remembered as one more well-meaning but failed messianic aspirant (cf. Acts 5:33-42).

---

1. Paul W. Meyer, *The Word in This World: Essays in New Testament Exegesis and Theology*, ed. John T. Carroll (Louisville, KY: Westminster John Knox Press, 2004), 23.

# The Stakes

But if God did raise Jesus from the grave as Jesus had anticipated (Matt. 12:38-40; 17:22-23; Mark 8:31-33; Luke 9:22; John 2:19), he thereby confirmed Jesus's witness regarding his Father (Acts 17:31). Jesus claimed his actions bore witness to his Father, not to himself (John 5:30-32; 8:48-54; 12:27-28; 17:1-5, 25-26).

Because of faith in Jesus, an untold number of martyrs have borne witness under intense persecution and torturous death. Because of their faith, Christians have constructed a vast, diverse institution called the church. They have developed definitive creeds and founded impressive institutions of higher learning and hospitals worldwide. Their faith has spawned an ethic founded upon Jesus's person and teachings. Through the centuries, Christianity has inspired monks and nuns to surrender their lives to contemplation and noble service to others. It has inspired persons gifted with keen intellects to develop impressive apologies (answers) for the faith. Christians have encouraged brilliant theologians to refine their faith into impressive systems. Christianity has motivated missionaries to risk life and limb to take the gospel of Jesus Christ around the world.

As admirable as all that might be, apart from Easter faith, Christians *as* Christians have nothing of substance to offer the world. Efforts to "preserve" Christian "pieces" as beneficial to humankind apart from Jesus's bodily resurrection are legion. Theologian Sarah Coakley observes that for many nineteenth-century liberal theologians Jesus's resurrection was a topic of "considerable embarrassment."[2] The "pieces" are deceptive and delusional (cf. 1 Cor. 15:12-19). As novelist Walker Percy observed, the Christian faith "stakes everything on a Person, an event existing here and now in time" and upon "News" about this Person.[3] Duke University New Testament scholar Richard Hays bluntly admits, "The resurrection is the

---

2. Sarah Coakley, *Christ Without Absolutes: A Study of the Christology of Ernst Troeltsch* (Oxford, UK: Clarendon Press, 1988), 174.

3. Walker Percy, *The Message in the Bottle* (New York: Farrar, Straus and Giroux, 1975), 140-44.

climactic element—indeed the linchpin—of the biblical story of God's redemption of the world. Without it the story falls apart."[4]

If the Father did raise his Witness (*martus*) from the grave (Acts 5:29-32; 1 Cor. 15:3-8; 1 Thess. 1:9-10), did not permit him to "see corruption" (decay, Acts 13:35), if he was truly "vindicated by the Spirit" (1 Tim. 3:16, NIV) "with power" (Rom. 1:4), then everything central to Jesus's kingdom-launching ministry, all the New Testament claims, is true and unavoidable. New Testament scholar Andy Johnson says that in Second Temple Judaism, resurrection and divine justice enacted as vindication were inseparably joined. In his resurrection, Jesus "experienced" justification, vindication for his faithful "obedience unto death" (cf. 1 Tim. 3:16).[5] The Father thereby confirmed that Jesus is "creation's rightful Lord" (see Phil. 2:9-11).[6]

If the Father raised his Son from the grave, adds Richard Hays, "then God is powerfully at work in the world in ways that defy common sense, redeeming the creation from its bondage to necessity and decay. That is precisely what the early Christians believed and proclaimed."[7] Jesus's resurrection, says N. T. Wright of Paul's consistent witness, means that God's new world has been inaugurated. The covenant will be renewed, sins will be forgiven, and death will be abolished.[8]

All conclusions and affirmations required by Jesus's resurrection must be honestly confronted, including that in the Spirit's power, Jesus faithfully revealed the Father. All that Jesus did and taught was vindicated by One more powerful than death. He must therefore be recognized as the bearer of truth and the defining model for obedience to God.[9]

---

4. Richard B. Hays, *Reading with the Grain of Scripture* (Grand Rapids: Eerdmans, 2020), 143.

5. Andy Johnson, "The Past, Present, and Future of Bodily Resurrection as Salvation: Christ, Church, and Cosmos," in *Cruciform Scripture: Cross, Participation, and Mission*, eds. Christopher Skinner, Nijay Gupta, Andy Johnson, and Drew Strait (Grand Rapids: Eerdmans, 2021), 210.

6. Ibid., 211.

7. Hays, *Reading with the Grain of Scripture*, 51.

8. N. T. Wright, *Surprised by Hope* (New York: HarperOne, 2008), 247-48.

9. Hays, *Reading with the Grain of Scripture*, 51.

Successive cultural developments, political and economic changes, advances in learning, and familiarity with other world religions have not dismissed or relaxed the requirement to recognize the universal implications and promise of Jesus's resurrection: "a *new reality has come to birth; a new way of being human* has been launched." That new reality is the "chain-breaking, idol-smashing, sin-abandoning power called [God's] 'forgiveness,' called 'utter gracious love,' called *Jesus*."[10]

As pivotal as Jesus's resurrection is for Christian faith, we must also recognize the importance of his life for the disciples and the early church. In her study of the Gospel of Mark, New Testament scholar Helen K. Bond shows how Mark intentionally expanded the Christian "gospel" so that it was no longer limited to Jesus's death and resurrection, but also included his life. Mark shapes a distinct identity for Jesus's followers. While Jesus is the unique Son of God and is filled with the Spirit, his countercultural way of life, as well as his death, must become normative for Christian discipleship.[11]

Methodist theologian Tom Greggs adds that in the life of Jesus we learn the meaning of true humanity, what God meant for humans to be all along. In the life of Jesus, we learn not only what our relationship to God should be but also what our relationship with one another should be. In Jesus's life we learn what it means to be created in God's image.[12]

## New Testament Claims

New Testament writers know that Christian faith rises or falls upon claims regarding Jesus's resurrection. The apostle Paul candidly admitted, "If Christ has not been raised, then our preaching is in vain and your faith is in vain. We are even found to be misrepresenting God" (1 Cor. 15:14-15, RSV). If Jesus was not raised from the dead, then faith in him is futile.

---

10. N. T. Wright, *The Day the Revolution Began: Reconsidering the Meaning of Jesus's Crucifixion* (San Francisco: HarperOne, 2016), 384-85.

11. Helen K. Bond, *The First Biography of Jesus: Genre and Meaning in Mark's Gospel* (Grand Rapids: Eerdmans, 2020), 5.

12. Tom Greggs, *The Breadth of Salvation: Rediscovering the Fullness of God's Saving Work* (Grand Rapids: Baker Academic, 2020), 43-46.

Those who trust in Jesus remain in their sins. If for this life alone believers have trusted Jesus, then they "are of all people most to be pitied" (v. 19).

The New Testament pulsates with an affirmation of Jesus's resurrection and recognizes the consequences had he not been. It is simply all or nothing. New Testament writers knew if God had indeed raised Jesus from the dead, something of universal and eternal importance had happened. In the words of Catholic scholar George Weigel, the risen Christ was believed to be "the axial point of the human saga."[13]

To better understand the early Christian affirmation regarding Jesus's resurrection, consider what Jesus's resurrection meant.[14]

*First*, early Christians meant that Jesus did in fact die. They and outside sources attest to the fact that the Romans crucified Jesus on a cross. The Romans knew how to eradicate their enemies. Crucifixion was one the most brutal forms of ancient torture. It often took several days before victims died of shock, exhaustion, and finally suffocation. Helen Bond makes a strong case for thinking Jesus was buried in shame. "As one condemned by a Jewish court, he could expect nothing better. . . . From start to finish, the burial was ignominious and dishonorable." For Jewish leaders, Jesus's shameful death was proof positive that he had not been God's spokesman.[15] The Nicene Creed is correct: Jesus was "dead and buried."

By contrast, the Qur'an (the book of Islam) says, "And they did not kill him, nor did they crucify him. . . . Rather, Allah raised him to Himself."[16]

*Second*, Jesus experienced resurrection,[17] not resuscitation, a new order of existence in which Jesus clearly retained his identity (John 20:19-28; 21:1-14). The marks of his passion were still evident (John 20:26-29). Lazarus was resuscitated, not resurrected (John 11:17-44). He would die

---

13. George Weigel, "Pope John Paul II's Soviet Spy," in *Wall Street Journal* (Opinion) (May 14, 2020). https://www.wsj.com/articles/pope-john-paul-iis-soviet-spy-11589498606?mod=opinion_lead_pos10.

14. Luke Timothy Johnson, *The Real Jesus: The Misguided Quest for the Historical Jesus and the Truth of the Traditional Gospels* (San Francisco: HarperSanFrancisco, 1996), 134-35.

15. Helen K. Bond, *The Historical Jesus: A Guide for the Perplexed* (New York: T. and T. Clark, 2012), 164-65.

16. The Holy Qur'an, 4:157-58.

17. See Bond, *The Historical Jesus*, for a detailed review of what resurrection meant for Jews after the exile (167-69).

again. Resuscitation produces astonishment but does not launch a religious movement as good news for all. It does not transform lives through the ages.[18]

The apostle Paul refers to Jesus's resurrection as "the first fruits of those who have died" (1 Cor. 15:20). Firstfruits were the first portion of a harvest. Paul explains that when Jesus returns, those who belong to him will be resurrected, transformed just as Jesus was (vv. 35 57).

*Third*, early Christians did not mean Jesus's "soul" had entered heavenly bliss, leaving his tortured body behind. Peter's Pentecost sermon explicitly affirms this (Acts 2:29-32). Jesus's whole person was the subject of resurrection, just as it will be for all Christians when the Lord returns (1 Cor. 15:51-57). Those who reduce salvation to "the soul" fail to understand the unbreakable bond between God the creator and God the redeemer (e.g., Rom. 8:18-25). Making the soul and not the body—the whole person—the object of redemption leads to abandoning the Christian hope of resurrection as set forth in the New Testament. It introduces a deterioration of the Christian faith.

## What the Disciples Knew

By affirming Jesus's resurrection, the disciples and other early Christians meant that on Easter morning, the third day after his death, God the Father confirmed that his Son shared his power, and could, through the Holy Spirit, transform and empower others (Acts 3:15; Rom. 6:4; 8:11; Eph. 1:20).[19] Not only did the resurrection happen to Jesus, through the power of the Holy Spirit (Rom. 1:4), but he could unleash resurrection power as "new creation" in his followers (John 3:1-8; Rom. 6:1; 2 Cor. 5:17). A new form of human life, shaped in the image of the resurrected Christ, could arise (Rom. 8:29; 1 Cor. 15; Gal. 4:19).[20]

Why did Jesus's disciples uniformly confess along with the apostle Thomas, "My Lord and my God!" (John 20:28)? Because in one instance after another, Jesus came to them, leaving no doubt about his identity

---

18. L. T. Johnson, *The Real Jesus*, 134.
19. Ibid.
20. Ibid.

(Matt. 28:9-20; Mark 16:9-20; Luke 24:13-49; John 20:11—21:23; 1 Cor. 15:3-8). George Weigel identifies all this as "the Easter Effect."[21]

Primary justification for making the Christian confession never changes. Discipleship and life-altering conviction come to birth in a transforming encounter with the risen Christ. Benedict XVI meant this in his encyclical, *Deus Caritas Est* [God Is Love]: "Being Christian is not the result of an ethical choice or a lofty idea, but the encounter with an event, a person, which gives life a new horizon and a decisive direction."[22]

In his letters, the apostle Paul clearly articulated the meaning of Jesus's cross and resurrection. He placed no value upon making the "foolishness" of the cross (1 Cor. 1:18) comprehensible to the "wise according to worldly standards" (v. 26, RSV). Echoing Paul, New Testament scholar Luke Timothy Johnson says, "To the wise of this world, Christianity has never been able to 'prove' its claims except by appeal to the experience and convictions of those already convinced."[23] Experience and conviction founded the Christian faith and continues to ground it now. The church, says Benedict XVI, "would not even have emerged and survived at all unless some extraordinary reality had preceded it."[24] The founding conviction and awareness "came directly from Jesus."[25] Danish Christian Søren Kierkegaard would have agreed. For authentic Christian faith to rise, the risen Christ must become our contemporary. Christian faith is either a resurrection-born conviction or it is hearsay, even if well-intended, eloquently argued, and diligently followed.[26]

Luke Johnson asks us to consider the unlikelihood of the Christian faith ever rising. Its founder had been executed as was customary for eliminating

21. George Weigel, "The Easter Effect and How It Changed the World," in *Wall Street Journal*, March 30, 2018. https://www.wsj.com/articles/the-easter-effect-and-how-it-changed -the-world-1522418701#comments_sector.

22. Benedict XVI (Joseph Ratzinger), *Deus Caritas Est*, Introduction, Vatican Website, December 25, 2005. http://www.vatican.va/content/benedict-xvi/en/encyclicals/documents /hf_ben-xvi_enc_20051225_deus-caritas-est.html.

23. L. T. Johnson, *The Real Jesus*, 168.

24. Benedict XVI, *Jesus of Nazareth* (New York: Image Books, 2007), 324.

25. Ibid.

26. Søren Kierkegaard, *Training in Christianity*, in *A Kierkegaard Anthology*, ed. Robert Bretall (Princeton, NJ: Princeton University Press, 1946), 409.

criminals who dared challenge Roman authority. Crucifixion was Rome's ultimate form of shaming, of saying, "Don't mess with Rome!" Execution by crucifixion was reserved primarily for the most vicious male criminals. Its purpose was to eliminate victims from consideration as humans. Jesus's disciples knew this. When his impending crucifixion became clear, they didn't stick around for an explanation. They were seized by "disorienting horror"[27] and fled in defeat, fear, and disillusionment (Mark 14:50). Peter even distanced himself by swearing he did not know Jesus (Matt. 26:74). It would be absurd to think these demoralized and fragmented people fabricated a "resurrection" in order to inaugurate a religion.

Creative imagination would not have endured or produced the results that followed. The risen Christ "stood among" the disciples. They were terrified, filled with fear (Gr., *emphoboi*, "they trembled"). Using the only explanation their culture provided, they thought they were seeing a ghost (a spirit, Luke 24:37).

## Encountering the Holy

What happened when the disciples encountered the risen Christ? They encountered the Holy God, the Wholly Other in his fullness, a reality attested in all the Gospels and Epistles. They saw clearly that in Jesus, God had fulfilled his promises to "Moses and all the prophets" (Luke 24:27; cf. Acts 3:17-26). Their encounter led to boldness, to action, to mission, to proclamation (Acts 4:5-12).

Jesus's presence was more powerful and commanding than before his crucifixion. His was the lasting presence of a personal, transcendent, and transforming power within the Christian community.[28] Jesus was not a past figure of fond remembrance, not a static moral teacher or exemplar, but the living Lord confessed and known in the community through the Holy Spirit, shaping the young church's identity, speaking through the

---

27. J. Louis Martyn, "A Personal Word," in Paul W. Meyer, *The Word in This World: Essays in New Testament Exegesis and Theology*, ed. John T. Carroll (Louisville, KY: Westminster John Knox Press, 2004), xxii.

28. Luke Timothy Johnson, *The Writings of the New Testament: An Interpretation* (Minneapolis: Fortress Press, 2010), 102.

church's prophets, teaching through its teachers, and healing through the hands of believers.[29]

Jesus interprets scripture (Luke 24:24, 46-47) and commissions his disciples to proclaim the news of his resurrection (Matt. 28:16-20; Luke 24:48). Peter and John told Jewish authorities in Jerusalem, "We cannot but speak of what we have seen and heard" (Acts 4:20, RSV). Empowerment for mission is made possible by Jesus's gift of the Holy Spirit (Luke 24:47-49; John 14:18-31). This is the same Spirit who raised Jesus from the grave (Rom. 8:11), who makes him present in the church, who effects new birth (John 3:1-15), resurrection (Rom. 6:1-4), and new creation (2 Cor. 5:17) in believers. "No one can say 'Jesus is Lord' except by the Holy Spirit" (1 Cor. 12:3).

Although only after Jesus's resurrection could the New Testament writers fully comprehend Jesus Christ as "God with us," his disciples had encountered the Holy God in Jesus during their pre-Easter walk with him. His "divine identity" repeatedly occurs in the Gospel narratives (e.g., Matt. 14:33; 17:5-6; Mark 6:45-52; 9:2-8; Luke 5:8; 9:28-36; John 1:14; 6:15-21). Mark records an instance in which the disciples hear an evil spirit call out to Jesus, "I know who you are, the Holy One of God" (Mark 1:24; see vv. 21-24). Luke Johnson brings together pre-Easter and post-Easter encounters. The resurrection experience of Jesus's power "threw constant light" on what the disciples experienced before Jesus's resurrection.[30]

Today only a holy encounter with the living Christ (as diverse as that might be), through the Holy Spirit, gives birth to faith and prompts a person to make the Christian confession (Acts 4:8-12).

## The Convincing Spirit

Christians can "bear witness." Only the Holy Spirit "can convince."

Jesus plainly told his disciples that "convincing" persons of who he is would be the work of the Holy Spirit (John 16:8-11; cf. 1 Cor. 12:3). Being "convinced" by the Spirit made, and makes, confession of faith possible and definitive. Being "convinced" by the Holy Spirit is a "surprising and

29. Ibid., 105.
30. Ibid., 112.

totally unexpected encounter that issues in mission."[31] Before then, Jesus Christ is a *question*; ever after he is the *ANSWER*.

How the Holy Spirit accomplishes this is a sovereign, divine prerogative, franchised to no Christian denomination. A Christian's role is to become a witnessing instrument in the process. John Wesley cautioned against "limiting the Almighty," for he "doeth whatsoever and whensoever it pleaseth him. He can convey his grace, either in or out of any of the means which he hath appointed."[32] "Convincing" might happen the first time a person hears the gospel proclaimed, or slowly as one learns and participates in the Christian narrative, or as a jolting revelation such as Saul of Tarsus experienced while journeying to Damascus to persecute Christians (Acts 9:1-22).

One of the most astonishing characteristics of Christian faith is how patiently and creatively the Holy Spirit leads persons to "hear" the gospel and confess Jesus Christ as Lord of all. The Spirit may utilize available symbols of a person's world, including those of another religion. The Spirit's current use of dreams, visions, and technology in Iran to bring about conversions and the growth of house churches illustrates the Spirit's craft.[33] Behind it all stands conviction, transforming awareness, that Jesus is risen from the grave. Do not seek "the living among the dead"! (Luke 24:5).

Christians "bear witness" as they tell the gospel story, live it faithfully, listen, and trust the Holy Spirit as the divine "convincer." So observed, the truth regarding Jesus Christ and human integrity are always safeguarded (2 Cor. 4:1-2). Much harm has been done to Christian witness because of failure to distinguish between "faithful witness" and "convincing." The warning is heard in the words of Pope John Paul II: "The Church . . . has

31. Ibid., 101.

32. John Wesley, "The Means of Grace," Sermon 16, pt. 5, sec. 4, *The Sermons of John Wesley*, Wesley Center Online. http://wesley.nnu.edu/john-wesley/the-sermons-of-john-wesley-1872-edition/sermon-16-the-means-of-grace/.

33. "What in the World Is God Doing in Iran?" (March 7, 2018), The Outreach Foundation. https://www.theoutreachfoundation.org/updates/2018/3/6/what-in-the-world-is-god-doing-in-iran.

no weapons at her disposal apart from those of the Spirit, of the word and of love."[34]

When the Holy Spirit "convinces," a person does not encounter an alien oppressor but an imminently recognizable and glorious source of freedom and human flourishing, a defining reality never before known to them—"eternal life" manifest and bestowed (John 1:4; 4:14; 1 John 1:1-4).

> *Love's redeeming work is done,*
> *fought the fight, the battle won.*
> *Death in vain forbids him rise;*
> *Christ has opened paradise.*
> *Alleluia, alleluia!*
> —Charles Wesley, 1707-88

---

34. John Paul II, *Redemptor hominis* [The Redeemer of Man]. The Vatican Website. http://www.vatican.va/content/john-paul-ii/en/encyclicals/documents/hf_jp-ii_enc_04031979_redemptor-hominis.html.

# 9

# THE MISSION OF GOD
## (*Missio Dei*)

## Introduction

Is God as parochial and punitive as parts of the Bible indicate? Does his plan favor Israel and exclude others? Will all people someday "serve" God through coerced submission to Israel as Isaiah promises (Isa. 14:2; 60:11-12)? Or as Richard Bauckham poses the question, do the Bible's claims for God's universality actually constitute a narrative of domination and oppression dressed up as universal benefit?[1] Does the Bible offer no more than another oppressive metanarrative of which this world has had its fill?[2]

If so, should those who respect and love all persons reject God? Should the Bible be retired and placed among other examples of oppressive re-

---

1. Richard Bauckham, *Bible and Mission: Christian Witness in a Postmodern World* (Grand Rapids: Baker Academic, 2003), 5-6.
2. Bauckham defines a metanarrative as "an attempt to grasp the meaning and destiny of human history as a whole by telling in a single story about it; to encompass, as it were, all the immense diversity of human stories in a single, overall story which integrates them into a single meaning" (*Bible and Mission*, 4). Philip Rieff succinctly stated the rejection of metanarratives as "an acute suspicion of all normative institutions" (*The Triumph of the Therapeutic: Uses of Faith after Freud* [New York: Harper and Row, 1966], 19).

ligious literature? Should Christians stop singing, "There's a wideness in God's mercy, / like the wideness of the sea"?

The Bible contains much that encourages portrayal of God as an ancient parochial deity who uses his power to favor those he loves and exclude those he hates. Consider: As the Hebrews prepare to invade an already occupied land, God commands, "As for the towns of these peoples that the LORD your God is giving you as an inheritance, you must not let anything that breathes remain alive. Indeed, you shall annihilate them—the Hittites and the Amorites, the Canaanites and the Perizzites, the Hivites and the Jebusites—just as the LORD your God has commanded" (Deut. 20:16-17; cf. Ps. 111:6).

Later, God commands King Saul, "Now go and attack Amalek, and utterly destroy all that they have; do not spare them, but kill both man and woman, child and infant, ox and sheep, camel and donkey" (1 Sam. 15:3). The psalmist thinks "the one who seizes [Babylon's] infants and dashes them against the rocks" will be happy; they are doing God's will (Ps. 137:9, NIV; see vv. 7-9).

One day, God promises Israel through Isaiah, all the merchandise of Egypt and Ethiopia will belong to Israel. The tall Sabeans will be placed in chains and become Israel's slaves. They will bow before Israel and declare, "God is with you alone, and . . . there is no [God] besides him" (Isa. 45:14).

God's apparent retribution against those he does not favor is not limited to the Old Testament. In the closing scenes of the New Testament, after all the talk in the Gospels about God's love, from the mouth of one called "Faithful and True" there issues a sharp sword with which he "smite[s] the nations." He then proceeds to rule them with a "rod of iron" (Rev. 19:15, RSV). He exhibits the full measure "of the fury of the wrath of God the Almighty" (v. 16; see vv. 11-16). After examining all this and more, theologian and philosopher Paul Copan asks, "Is God a vindictive bully?"[3]

If this is the God of the Bible, are morally responsible people duty-bound to reject him? Can he be commended to people who adhere

---

3. Paul Copan, *Is God a Vindictive Bully?: Reconciling Portrayals of God in the Old and New Testaments* (Grand Rapids: Baker Academic, 2022).

to religions other than Judaism and Christianity? Should the Christian faith dare lift its head above any other aggressive and oppressive religious sentiment?

Not surprisingly, readers might be struck by an apparent discrepancy between these questions and what follows regarding the mission of God. There are no simple resolutions. Historical and cultural contexts provide some explanation, but not all. For Christians, the final resolution resides in their affirmation that in his person—his life, death, and resurrection—Jesus Christ is the definitive revelation of the Father. He alone is how they measure and understand the Old Testament. He is God's Word (John 1:1-5) spoken in creation and redemption. In him all God's promises are fulfilled (2 Cor. 1:20). Two of Jesus's disciples were perplexed as they walked to Emmaus on the day of his resurrection. The risen Christ joined them and soon began to resolve their confusion. "Beginning with Moses and all the prophets," Jesus "interpreted to them the things about himself in all the scriptures" (Luke 24:27). In him alone may we see definitively manifest God's self-giving love for all persons and cultures (Eph. 1:3-10). He makes it possible, says Richard Bauckham, to see the Bible as a "project aimed at the kingdom of God, that is, towards the achievement of God's purposes for good in the whole of God's creation."[4] The Bible's mission narrative proceeds from the particular to the universal,[5] toward the creation of an "ever-new people."[6] Joseph Ratzinger (Pope Benedict XVI) urges us to read the Old and New Testaments "with Christ and in Christ . . . in whom all things have been fulfilled and in whom all [the Bible's] validity and truth are revealed."[7]

## The Missionary God

When we read the Bible as Joseph Ratzinger counsels, we see that it predominantly reveals a missionary God whose love and redemption are universal. He intends to redeem his creation. God's promise to Abraham

4. Bauckham, *Bible and Mission*, 11.
5. Ibid.
6. Ibid., 15.
7. Pope Benedict XVI (Joseph Ratzinger), *In the Beginning: A Catholic Understanding of the Story of Creation and the Fall*, trans. Boniface Ramsey (Grand Rapids: Eerdmans, 1990), 16.

is that "in you all the families of the earth [will] be blessed" (Gen. 12:3; 18:18; 22:18). On two occasions, the promise to bless the nations is given through Abraham's son Isaac (26:4) and grandson Jacob (28:14). Read carefully, Genesis strongly suggests that blessing the families of the earth will be the goal of the biblical story, even though much of the Old Testament only echoes the promise.[8] The apostle Paul says in the promise to Abraham, God "preached the gospel beforehand" (Gal. 3:8, RSV). Jesus Christ, one specific descendant of Abraham, brings blessing to Israel and all the families of the earth (Gal. 3:6-9, 16). In radical contrast to all that is punitive, parochial, and exclusive, the God whom we encounter in the Bible "pins [his] mission statement to every signpost on the way."[9]

From Genesis to Revelation, we meet an astonishing God who patiently gives himself for covenant, for communion, for fulfilling his intention as Creator. Always taking the redemptive initiative, God refuses to give up. A prevailing theme in the Old and New Testaments is God's steadfast and everlasting love (*chesed* [*hesed*]: mercy, goodness, kindness, faithfulness; appears well over two-hundred times).[10] This is God whose mission we are considering. He is YAHWEH, the Holy One of Israel who wills to be known and will be known to the ends of the earth. He is the same God who is Father, Son, and Holy Spirit, the one Jesus addressed as Abba, Father (Mark 14:36).

## The Bible's Grand Narrative

The Bible shows God acting in surprising ways to redeem the nations. It discloses God's grand narrative. Christopher Wright identifies four parts to God's universal mission: (1) The Bible opens with the account of creation. God is working toward a goal and completing it with satisfaction. (2) It moves on to the conflict and problem caused by humankind's rebellion

---

8. Bauckham, *Bible and Mission*, 30.

9. Christopher J. H. Wright, *The Mission of God: Unlocking the Bible's Grand Narrative* (Downers Grove, IL: IVP Academic, 2006), 23.

10. John H. Walton says that "in contrast, it is difficult to find [any affirmation of faithfulness] for the gods of the ancient Near East. Words that convey loyalty are never used of the gods in that way. The gods have no agreement or promises to be faithful to and no obligations or commitments to fulfill" (*Ancient Near Eastern Thought and the Old Testament* [Grand Rapids: Baker Academic, 2006], 109).

against God's purposes. (3) Most of its narrative reveals God's redemptive purposes being worked out on the stage of human history, including fulfillment of all his promises in the Son of God, Jesus Christ (2 Cor. 1:19-20). And (4) the Bible concludes beyond the horizon of its story with the consummation of new creation inaugurated by Jesus's resurrection.[11]

The Bible's clear promise is that God will ultimately redeem his creation. God's grace and patience are strikingly prominent in his grand narrative. He is reconciling the world to himself through self-emptying, sacrificial love (2 Cor. 5:19; Phil. 2:7).

God's designs included persons who were not part of physical Abrahamic identity, for example: Cyrus the Persian ruler (Isa. 44:24—45:13), a Roman centurion (Matt. 8:5-13), a Syrophoenician woman (Mark 7:24-30), and "foreigners" in Jesus's genealogy (Matt. 1:1-17).

God's grand narrative climaxes in Jesus who is the Christ (Messiah). He is the incarnate embodiment of God's mission to the world, God's good news for all people. At his baptism by John the Baptist, a voice came from heaven, "You are my Son, the Beloved; with you I am well pleased" (Mark 1:11). In his first recorded sermon, empowered by the Holy Spirit, Jesus proclaimed good news for captives, healing for the blind, and liberty for the oppressed (Luke 4:16-19; Isa. 61:1-2). He is God's agent of redemption for all the earth (Isa. 49:6). In Jesus, God's risen and ascended Christ, the Light of the World (John 8:12), God is now reconciling the world to himself (2 Cor. 5:19; Eph. 1:3-10). Jesus commissions and accompanies his witnesses as bearers of God's good news (Matt. 28:16-20).

## The Old Testament Testimony

The Historical Books, the Psalms, and the Prophets predominantly testify to God's universal mission of redemption. We are identifying what is predominant and are not attempting to resolve questions posed by apparent contradictions of God's grand strategy.

---

11. C. Wright, *The Mission of God*, 63-64.

## The Historical Books

### Exodus

In Exodus 9:13-16 God tells Pharaoh he has been raised up so God's "name might be declared throughout the earth" (v. 16, RSV). Yahweh (3:14-15) is no local, finite deity seeking victory over another local deity. He is the universal God who will be known in all the earth (cf. Ps. 78:3-4; Isa. 43:12). God's purpose is larger than freeing Hebrew slaves (Rom. 9:17).

In Exodus 19:5-6, God instructs Moses to tell the escaped Hebrews, "If you obey my voice and keep my covenant, you shall be my own possession among all peoples; for all the earth is mine, and you shall be to me a kingdom of priests and a holy nation" (RSV). This text is the hinge between the exodus (chs. 1—18), making the covenant, giving the Law, and constructing the wilderness tabernacle. It combines imperative (how Israel is to live before God) and promise (what Israel should become among the nations). The promise is universal. God has not forgotten his wider mission of blessing all people, his purpose for all the earth.[12] Israel is commissioned for that purpose.

### Kings

During the temple's dedication, part of Solomon's prayer (1 Kings 8:41-43, 60-61; Num. 23:8-10) is for foreigners who do not belong to Yahweh's people. They come from a distant land to pray, for they have learned of his great name, his mighty hand, and his outstretched arm. When foreigners pray, Solomon asks, may God hear and answer their petitions "so that all the peoples of the earth may know your name and fear you, as do your own people Israel" (1 Kings 8:43, NIV; see vv. 41-43). He asks that "all the peoples of the earth may know that the Lord is God and that there is no other" (v. 60, NIV). The temple is the true spiritual home for all people. Wright observes that among the historical books, here the universal vision is most remarkably expressed.[13]

---

12. Ibid., 234-35.
13. Ibid., 229.

Israel is central to God's mission. It must be "fully committed to the LORD [their] God, to live by his decrees and obey his commands" (v. 61, NIV). Otherwise, the blessing of foreigners and a spreading knowledge of YAHWEH would not occur.

## The Psalms

The eventual universal worship of God is boldly expressed in Psalm 22:27-28: "All the ends of the earth shall remember and turn to the LORD; and all the families of the nations shall worship before him. For dominion belongs to the LORD, and he rules over the nations."

Psalm 47:9 declares all the nations belong to God, "The princes of the peoples gather as the people of the God of Abraham." The nations will become one with the people of Abraham.

Psalm 67:1-2 asks that God's "way" and his salvation be known "among all nations." Here the Aaronic prayer of Num. 6:22-27 has been turned into a prayer for the nations. The blessings of salvation beforehand enjoyed by Israel should now be showered upon all people. "Let the nations be glad and sing for joy, for you judge the peoples with equity" (Ps. 67:4).

## The Prophets

In the prophets the universal mission of God comes to full Old Testament expression and anticipation.

### Isaiah

In what Wright identifies as "one of the most breathtaking announcements of any prophets" and missiologically the most significant of all Old Testament texts,[14] Isaiah anticipates that "in that day Israel will be the third with Egypt and Assyria, a blessing in the midst of the earth, whom the LORD of hosts has blessed, saying, 'Blessed be Egypt my people, and Assyria the work of my hands, and Israel my heritage'" (19:24-25, RSV). Israel will no longer be the exclusive transmitter of God's blessing. Its identity will be merged with that of Egypt and Assyria, Israel's former oppressors. The Abrahamic promise is fulfilled not only in them but *through*

---

14. Ibid., 236.

them. Not only will foreign nations experience God's blessing, along with Israel they will *become* a blessing for all the earth.[15]

In Isaiah, God again promises his universal reign by using picturesque language:

> On this mountain the LORD of hosts will make for all peoples a feast of fat things, a feast of wine on the lees, of fat things full of marrow, of wine on the lees well refined. And he will destroy on this mountain the covering that is cast over all peoples, the veil that is spread over all nations. He will swallow up death for ever, and the Lord GOD will wipe away tears from all faces, and the reproach of his people he will take away from all the earth; for the LORD has spoken. (25:6-8, RSV; cf. 2:1-5)

Isaiah assures us that ultimately God will remove from human life the curse of death (cf. Rev. 21:14). Isaiah's promise—"he will swallow up death for ever" (Isa. 25:8, RSV)—applies to "all peoples" and "all nations" (v. 7, RSV). In the New Testament, Paul connects the promise of God through Abraham to the victory of Jesus's resurrection over death's reign in the world. Christ's triumph will be for all people (Rom. 4:16-17; 5:12-21).[16]

Old Testament scholar Bernhard Anderson observes that Second Isaiah's perspective (chs. 40—66)[17] "is as wide as the Creation and as long as the whole sweep of history."[18] Isaiah announces that Israel's redemption from exile will be part of the redemption of all the nations. Isaiah 45:22-23 is a classic expression of this promise, "Turn to me and be saved, all the ends of the earth! For I am God, and there is no other. . . . 'To me every knee shall bow, every tongue shall swear.'" This text appears amid chapters where the errors of idolatry have been exposed and so-called

15. Ibid.

16. Ibid., 237.

17. The second half of Isaiah (chs. 40—66) is written from the perspective of Babylonian exile. Many scholars divide the book even further by attributing chapters 56—66 to a Third Isaiah. They observe that Third Isaiah speaks to exiles who have returned and begun the difficult task of reconstructing the temple. It begins (56:1-8) with inclusive promises to "foreigners" and "eunuchs." The promises apply to those who become Jews.

18. Bernhard W. Anderson, *Understanding the Old Testament*, 3rd ed. (Englewood Cliffs, NJ: Prentice-Hall, 1975), 454.

gods of the nations have been defeated. But God's ultimate purpose is the salvation of the nations, not their ridicule and destruction.

*Jeremiah*

Jeremiah lays down a shocking condition for all nations to be blessed and glorify God: "If you return, O Israel, says the LORD, . . . if you remove your abominations from my presence . . . , and if you swear, 'As the LORD lives!' in truth, in justice, and in uprightness, *then* nations shall be blessed by you, and by you they shall boast" (Jer. 4:1-2; emphasis added). True repentance by Israel would have far-reaching consequences for itself, and also for the "nations." This text sheds full light on God's problem people. Not only were they an affront to God, but they were a hindrance to his mission to the nations as well.[19]

*Jonah*

Jonah is a book-length declaration that all people, including enemies of the Jews, are included in God's mercy and care. His love extends far beyond the chosen community. When the policies of Nehemiah and Ezra were promoting an exclusive nationalism among the returning exiles, Jonah declared that Israel is called to bear witness to a God whose salvation extends to the ends of the earth. Like Isaiah, Jonah represents "prophetic universalism."[20]

# The New Testament Testimony

## Matthew

The Gospel of Matthew accents Jesus's universal importance. The Abrahamic and Davidic covenants are combined. Matthew introduces Jesus as the son of David *and* the son of Abraham (1:1). As the son of Abraham, Jesus will fulfill promises to Abraham's seed: blessing for the nations. As the son of David, Jesus will fulfill the promised messianic reign over all the earth.

---

19. C. Wright, *The Mission of God*, 241.
20. Anderson, *Understanding the Old Testament*, 564.

Israel's special calling was to bear God's light to the nations (Matt. 2:1-2; 12:15-21; Isa. 42:1-4). The mission is being fulfilled in and by Jesus.[21] In him, the light for the world is dawning (Matt. 4:12-16). Jesus is the Messiah, the promised one, not only for the Jews but also for the Gentiles. The latter is anticipated in Jesus's genealogy (28:29), which includes four women (Tamar, Rahab, Ruth, and Bathsheba [1:3-6]) regarded as non-Israelites. It is explicitly affirmed in "the Great Commission" (28:16-20).

Matthew describes the anticipated climactic messianic banquet in the kingdom of heaven as a time when Gentiles will be seated with the patriarchs (8:11-13; cf. 22:1-14). The promise appears immediately after Jesus commends the faith of a Roman centurion as superior to any he has observed in Israel (8:10). Clearly, the kingdom of God arriving in Jesus breaks down traditional barriers that obstructed the promise of universal inclusion made to Abraham. The gospel of the kingdom is based upon faith alone; it removes all traditional barriers.[22] For example, Jesus angered Pharisees by abolishing traditional food restrictions that had fortified separation between Jews and Gentiles (15:10-20; cf. Mark 9:19).

Matthew concludes by emphasizing the universality of Jesus Christ and the worldwide call to discipleship.[23] Jesus instructs his emissaries regarding how the original Abrahamic commission (Gen. 12:1-3) is to be fulfilled: "Go therefore and make disciples of all nations, baptizing them in the name of the Father and of the Son and of the Holy Spirit" (Matt. 28:19).

## Luke

The songs of Mary (Luke 1:46-55) and Zechariah (vv. 68-79) thank God for renewing his mercy to Israel. They recognize God is fulfilling his promise to Abraham (vv. 55, 73). Luke announces the universal significance of the salvation arriving in Jesus. Simeon takes the baby Jesus in his arms and realizes he is looking at God's promised salvation (2:30). In Jesus he recognizes good news for "all peoples, a light for revelation to the Gentiles, and for glory to thy people Israel" (vv. 31-32, RSV).

---

21. Richard B. Hays, *Echoes of Scripture in the Gospels* (Waco, TX: Baylor University Press, 2016), 175.

22. C. Wright, *The Mission of God*, 244.

23. Ibid.

Luke concludes on the same universal note as Matthew. "Then [Jesus] opened their minds to understand the Scriptures, and said to them, 'Thus it is written, that the Christ should suffer and on the third day rise from the dead, and that repentance and forgiveness of sins should be preached in his name to all nations, beginning from Jerusalem'" (24:45-47, RSV). The blessing promised to Abraham will be fulfilled in the name of Jesus, crucified by his enemies but raised by the power of God.

## John

Richard Hays thinks Jesus's statement, "I have other sheep that are not of this sheep pen. I must bring them also" (John 10:16, NIV), suggests a "universal dimension to the saving significance of Jesus' death."[24] The suggestion is that Jesus is referring to *Gentiles* who will hear Jesus's voice and become members of his flock. This interpretation is consistent with John's presentation of Jesus as the Word of God (John 1:1-5) through whom all creatures came into being and in whom they find life and light.[25]

New Testament scholar Sherri Brown maintains that in John, receiving and abiding with the risen Christ constitute a mandate for mission to the world; the mission entails loving the world as Jesus did. Mission will be "sustained by participating in the indwelling relationship of God as Father, Son, and advocating Spirit."[26] Brown explains that participating in divine life and love is inseparable from participating in God's life-giving mission in the world.[27]

## Acts

The Book of Acts (3:1-26) tells of a lame man being healed in the temple. Peter asked, "Fellow Israelites, why does this surprise you? Why do you stare at us as if by our own power or godliness we had made this man walk?" (v. 12, NIV). Peter explained the man had been healed because of his faith in the risen Lord. Peter's response connects the healing to Abra-

---

24. Ibid., 342.

25. Ibid.

26. Sherri Brown, "'Follow Me': The Mandate for Mission in the Gospel of John," in *Cruciform Scripture*, 182.

27. Ibid., 164. Brown is drawing upon Michael Gorman, *Abide and Go: Missional Theosis in the Gospel of John* (Eugene, OR: Cascade, 2018), 8.

ham. God said to Abraham, "Through your offspring all peoples on earth will be blessed" (v. 25, NIV). Peter's hearers were physical descendants of Abraham. But they had not yet entered the "blessing of Abraham" fulfilled in Jesus Messiah. Entry is gained through repentance and faith in the name of Jesus (2:16). Conditions for entrance have become universal (2:16).[28]

## Paul

New Testament scholar Michael J. Gorman says according to Paul, God is on a mission to liberate all people from sin and death (Rom. 8:2). God's mission has been gloriously inaugurated in Jesus Messiah. In confident hope, we await its consummation. This is the prophetically promised new creation (v. 21). God is even now fulfilling his mission, implementing liberation through the sin-defeating and life-giving death and resurrection of Jesus. God is accomplishing this for all people and for the entire cosmos (vv. 18-25).[29]

All over the eastern Mediterranean, Paul diligently preached that in Jesus Christ, God had fulfilled all promises made to Abraham, Moses, and the prophets (Rom. 15:8-12; 2 Cor. 1:19-22). Christ is the mystery of God now fully revealed (Rom. 10:25; 1 Cor. 2:7; Eph. 3:9; Col. 1:26 ff.). Already, the existence of Jews and Gentiles together, through the gospel of peace, is a "substantive sign that the eschatological age of shalom," the "ingathering of the nations to worship God" has begun in Jesus the Messiah (Gal. 6:15-16; Eph. 2:14-17).[30]

On this conviction Paul forged his theology and missionary practice. His letters are filled with the new situation's universality. Paul told the Galatians, "All of you who were baptized into Christ have clothed yourselves with Christ. There is neither Jew nor Gentile, neither slave nor free, nor is there male and female, for you are all one in Christ Jesus" (Gal. 3:27-28, NIV). To the Romans he said, "This righteousness is given through faith in Jesus Christ to all who believe. There is no difference between Jew and

---

28. C. Wright, *The Mission of God*, 246.
29. Michael J. Gorman, *Becoming the Gospel: Paul, Participation, and Mission* (Grand Rapids: Eerdmans, 2015), 24.
30. Michael J. Gorman, *The Death of the Messiah and the Birth of the New Covenant* (Eugene, OR: Cascade Books, 2014), 142.

Gentile" (Rom. 3:22, NIV). To the Corinthians he declared, "We were all baptized by one Spirit so as to form one body—whether Jews or Gentiles, slave or free—and we were all given the one Spirit to drink" (1 Cor. 12:13, NIV; cf. Eph. 2:12-14).

For Paul, Abraham's "obedience of faith" constituted his response to God's command and promise; it is the standard from all people and nations (e.g., Rom. 10:12-13; Gal. 3:8, 26-29). In Romans 1:5 (repeated at the letter's end) Paul says, "Through [Jesus Christ] we have received grace and apostleship to bring about the obedience of faith for the sake of his name among all the nations" (RSV). This defines Paul's apostolic assignment. Gentiles who were coming to Christ are full participants in the new covenant.

> Now in Christ Jesus you who once were far away have been brought near by the blood of Christ. For he himself is our peace, who has made the two groups one and has destroyed the barrier, the dividing wall of hostility, by setting aside in his flesh the law with its commands and regulations. His purpose was to create in himself one new humanity out of the two, thus making peace, and in one body to reconcile both of them to God through the cross, by which he put to death their hostility. (Eph. 2:13-16, NIV)

New Testament scholar Dean Flemming says Paul contextualized his sermons for each audience. Luke records two of Paul's sermons to Gentiles. Acts 14:15-17 is a "mini-sermon" to the citizens of Lystra imbedded in Greek popular religion.[31] To correct them, Paul builds a bridge between the one true God and how God has already manifested his presence among them. In times past, God let nations "go their own way." But "he has not left himself without testimony." He has graciously "shown kindness by giving you rain from heaven and crops in their seasons; he provides you with plenty of food and fills your hearts with joy" (vv. 16-17, NIV). The one true God is not an intruding stranger. Although the Lystrans have not known it, all along God has been acting for them, setting the stage for their hearing the gospel.

---

31. Dean Flemming, *Recovering the Full Mission of God: A Biblical Perspective on Being, Doing and Telling* (Downers Grove, IL: IVP Academic, 2013), 140.

Paul's address to Athenian intellectuals (probably for two hours)[32] in the Areopagus in late AD 50 or early 51 (Acts 17:16-34) is thorough and nuanced, "exquisitely adapted to his audience,"[33] which included Stoic and Epicurean philosophers. N. T. Wright says Paul was being charged with bringing foreign divinities into Athens.[34] He was in the presence of the "supreme court" in the center of ancient culture. Paul defended his message and engaged primary tenets of the Greek worldview. Things could have gone badly.[35]

The address begins with Paul establishing rapport. He notes that among all their other deities, the Athenians have an altar "to an unknown god" (v. 23), the one Paul is now proclaiming, making him known. God has now fully revealed himself to humankind in Jesus Christ, whom God raised from the dead (vv. 30-31). Echoing John (1:9), Paul says that without realizing it, already the Athenian philosophers "live and move and have [their] being" in God, who is "not far from each one of us" (Acts 17:28, 27).

Instead of coarsely refuting the religious beliefs of his audience, Flemming tells us Paul "engages his listeners' beliefs and worldviews in a way that both connects and confronts. . . . He expresses biblical revelation in language and categories that would strike a chord with his listeners."[36] He is sensitive to the beliefs of his Athenian audience while clearly declaring the God of the Scriptures in a manner that resonated with them.[37] Without confusing the gospel with pagan concepts, Paul used language of the philosophers to serve the gospel.

Following Paul's example, while preserving the purity of the gospel without falling into religious syncretism, wise messengers will discern how the gracious God has been on the scene and active long before they arrived.

32. N. T. Wright, *Paul: A Biography* (New York: HarperOne, 2018), 195.
33. Flemming, *Recovering the Full Mission*, 141.
34. N. T. Wright and Bird, *The New Testament in Its World*, 640.
35. N. T. Wright, *Paul: A Biography*, 104-5.
36. Flemming, *Recovering the Full Mission*, 141.
37. Ibid., 141-42.

Jesus's messengers should be "bridge builders," not "wrecking crews." They must be equipped for genuine dialogue, marked by knowledge of the Christian faith, *and* of the religious context in which they minister. Paul was informed regarding the beliefs and culture of his audiences. He modeled "a patient and respectful approach to evangelism."[38] He demonstrated "creative flexibility and courageous fidelity to the apostolic gospel."[39]

## Revelation

The Book of Revelation is the climactic vision of the Bible, "the omega point of the long sweep of covenantal history."[40] Revelation restates and expands God's plan to redeem the world and lead all people to know and worship him. At history's culmination stands a kingdom composed of ransomed people drawn "from every tribe and language and people and nation." Moreover, they are priests in service to God (Rev. 5:10; see vv. 9-10). Gloriously covenantal in character, Revelation pictures God at home among his people as the crowning achievement of his redemptive mission.[41] The nations will finally live by the light of the Lamb of God who takes away the sins of the world (Rev. 21:23-24).

Revelation 4—7 offers a comprehensive vision of the entire universe from the perspective of God's throne. The vision is "neck-stretching [and] mind-boggling."[42] The cross of Christ is the key; it unlocks the purpose and meaning of history.

Dean Flemming offers a significant restatement of how to understand Revelation. Instead of viewing the book through *predictive lenses* that see it as God's "game plan for the end time," we should see "how Revelation bears witness to God's massive mission to redeem and restore the whole creation—including people—through Christ, the slain and risen Lamb. Revelation shows us the ultimate goal of God's loving purpose for the world, which is 'making everything new'" (Rev. 21:5). Moreover, Revelation "seeks to equip and energize God's people to get caught up in what

---

38. Ibid., 143.
39. Ibid.
40. C. Wright, *The Mission of God*, 356.
41. Ibid., 355-56.
42. Ibid., 249.

God is doing to bring about wholeness and redemption to the world."[43] It calls Christians to bear witness to God's great purposes, to God's redeeming mission with their lips and with their lives.[44]

Against all expectations, God will fulfill his universal mission of healing and redemption through a wounded Lamb. The Lamb "unlocks God's magnificent plan to redeem every tribe and nation," not by threat and coercion, but "precisely because he suffers and dies" (Rev. 5:9-10).[45]

From the scattering of the nations in Genesis (11:1-9) we have arrived at God's healing of the nations in Revelation (21:1-6). Wright notes that chapters 21—22 of Revelation combine imagery from all the covenants of Scripture: Noah, Abraham, Moses, and David. "And the New Covenant is there in the fact that all this will be accomplished by the blood of the Lamb who was slain."[46]

How the nations will be brought to worship of and obedience to YAH-WEH remains a mystery (Rom. 11:33-36). But the divine director of his own cosmic drama intends eventually to bring the Gentile observers out of their seats "and onto the stage to join the original cast."[47] Christopher Wright conceives a sequel to the drama's finale. Amid resounding praises, God "will turn to Abraham and say, 'There you are. I kept my promises. Mission accomplished.'"[48]

## Inevitable Questions

After Jesus's resurrection the disciples asked, "Lord, are you at this time going to restore the kingdom to Israel?" Jesus answered, "It is not for you to know the times or dates the Father has set by his own authority" (Acts 1:6-7, NIV).

---

43. Dean Flemming, "Revelation Is Good News for Today, Not a Game Plan for the Future," *Christianity Today* (September 2022), 66. Flemming has extensively developed this theme in *Foretaste of the Future: Reading Revelation in Light of God's Mission* (Downers Grove, IL: IVP Academic, 2022).

44. Dean Flemming, *Foretaste of the Future: Reading Revelation in Light of God's Mission* (Downers Grove, IL: IVP Academic, 2022), 22.

45. Flemming, "Revelation Is Good News," 68.

46. C. Wright, *The Mission of God*, 356.

47. Ibid., 489.

48. Ibid., 251.

Many Christians share the disciples' questions: *"When* will the kingdom be fulfilled? When will Jesus Christ become the Light of the World in history?" Through the ages Christians have repeated the saints' question posed in Revelation 6:10: "How long, Sovereign Lord, holy and true?" (NIV). Given endless conflicts between races and cultures, brutality visited upon the vulnerable in worldwide sex trafficking, and a thriving abortion industry, the questions become more intense.

The answer? "We don't know."

The almost endless diversity of religious allegiances, illustrated for instance by the millions of Hindus in India who worship the River Ganges as a goddess, punctuates the answer. And given the shamefully fragmented condition of Christianity, what is there about the Christian faith that would encourage anyone to hope for the Kingdom's universal fulfillment? The same question can be asked because of brutal persecution Christians are enduring in many parts of the world. In Iraq, for example, largely because of fierce persecution, the number of Christians declined from 1.5 million before 2003 to about 150,000 in 2019. Within one generation, Iraq's Christian population shrunk by more than 90 percent.[49]

Additional chapters would be required to deal with the obstacles to God's mission created by persecution of Jews by Christians, brought about in part by the church's "tragic history of overlooking or even severing the gospel's roots [from] the history of Israel."[50] Honest treatment would require exposing elimination of Jews by Christians during the Medieval Crusades, butchery of thousands of Spanish Jews in the late fourteenth century, forced conversions in the fifteenth century, persecution unleashed by Martin Luther, and Christian Europe forcing Jews into ghettos in the eighteenth century. German church compliance with Adolph Hitler and the Holocaust constitutes a singular scandal.

---

49. Ines A. Murzaku, "Persecuted and Forgotten? Defending Defenseless Christians," The Catholic Thing, December 28, 2019. https://www.thecatholicthing.org/2019/12/28 /persecuted-and-forgotten-defending-defenseless-Christians/?utm_source=The +Catholic+Thing+Daily&utm_campaign=12e43d414d-EMAIL_CAMPAIGN _2018_12_07_01_02_COPY_02&utm_medium=email&utm_term=0_769a14e16a-12e43d41 4d-244109025.

50. Hays, *Echoes of Scripture*, 363.

The horrible and cautionary record of cruelty visited upon others in the name of Jesus Christ is ineradicable; it must never disappear from Christian memory and confession.

The decline and virtual obliteration of thriving Christian communities, highly developed ecclesiastical structures, and the work of stellar theologians in Asia, the Middle East, and Africa brought on by Muslim conquests in the seventh century AD pose their own bewildering questions.[51]

However, there was little in the first century BC that would have prompted anyone to expect an angel would soon appear to a virgin girl named Mary to announce she would be the mother of the long-awaited Messiah. No one could have predicted God would act in that way. But Mary, Elisabeth, Zechariah, and Simeon had trusted, eagerly waiting for the Redeemer to come and rescue Israel (Luke 2:25-35).

Jesus's instructions for the church today are the same as on the day of his ascension: "Tarry until you have been empowered by the Holy Spirit. Then go and be my witnesses to the ends of the earth—to the nations." The Holy Spirit empowered the disciples, and obedient faith sent them as witnesses to "the ends of the earth." The missional pattern has never changed—resurrection confidence and hope, Spirit empowerment, and faithful witness.

> *I cannot tell how he will win the nations,*
> *How he will claim his earthly heritage,*
> *How satisfy the needs and aspirations*
> *Of east and west, of sinner and of sage.*
> *But this I know, all flesh shall see his glory,*
> *And he shall reap the harvest he has sown,*
> *And some glad day his sun will shine in splendor*
> *When he the Savior, Savior of the world, is known.*
> —W. Y. Fullerton [c. 1920], "I Cannot Tell"

---

51. Philip Jenkins, *The Lost History of Christianity: The Thousand-Year Golden Age of the Church of the Middle East, Africa, and Asia—and How It Died* (New York: HarperOne, 2009).

# Conclusion

To conclude, consider what sort of people Christians must be in order to bear faithful witness to the God who in Christ is "blessing the nations."

*First*, before participating in mission, Christians must, with the apostle Thomas, confess "My Lord and my God" (John 20:28). They must "know" (17:3) the identity of the true, living God as fully manifest in the crucified and risen Jesus.

Knowing who Christ is, is inseparable from being transformed by him, "delivered . . . from the dominion of darkness and transferred . . . to the kingdom of [God's] beloved Son" (Col. 1:13, RSV). As Karl Barth notes, revelation happens in the *event* of reconciliation (justification and sanctification) in Jesus Christ, through the Holy Spirit. Revelation "declares itself" in "conscious, intelligent, living, grateful, willing and active participation in its occurrence."[52] Only such a "knowing" church can be entrusted with "mak[ing] disciples of all nations" (Matt. 28:19).

For many Christians, such as the countless number of Christian leaders in China who have been imprisoned because of their fidelity to Jesus Christ, "knowing" who Jesus is will result in intense persecution, even death.

*Second*, Christians must understand the "good news" of Jesus Christ: in his life, death, and resurrection, God has launched his long-anticipated kingdom on earth (Mark 1:14-15). Christians must know the gospel as a universal invitation to repent and enter God's reign, to experience "new creation" through the power of Christ (2 Cor. 5:17-18). In the Spirit's power, Christians must believe and act upon the fact that in Christ "God was pleased to reconcile to himself all things" (Col. 1:20).

Richard Bauckham summarizes succinctly: "The Gospel is that in Jesus Christ the curse has been set aside and God's creative purpose for the blessing of his creation is established beyond any possibility of reversal. God's last and effective word is his blessing . . . spoken in the life, death and resurrection of Jesus."[53]

---

52. Karl Barth, *Church Dogmatics*, vol. 4, *The Doctrine of Reconciliation*, pt. 3.1, trans. G. W. Bromiley (Edinburgh: T. and T. Clark, 2004), 8.

53. Bauckham, *Bible and Mission*, 36.

*Third*, "knowing" who Christ is, is inseparable from an ethic that evidences Christ as Lord of all. The ethical challenge before God's people is to live in ways that express and facilitate God's reign.[54] This means walking in the way of the Lord (Col. 1:8-12). Richard Bauckham adds that remaining faithful to the Lord in mission steadfastly excludes the church being co-opted "by the ideology of any of the other forces at work in the world."[55]

> *Word of life, most pure and strong,*
> *Word for which the nations long,*
> *Spread abroad until from night*
> *All the world awakes to light.*
> —J. F. Bahnmaier, 1744—1841

---

54. C. Wright, *The Mission of God*, 357.
55. Bauckham, *Bible and Mission*, 112.

# 10
# WHAT'S "HISTORICAL" ABOUT JESUS? (Part 1)

The Christian faith is grounded in Jesus of Nazareth who lived and died in Palestine during the early first century AD. Christians affirm that the One Creator God became fully incarnate in him without compromising his humanity, that in him God inaugurated his earthly reign as good news for all, that after his crucifixion by the Romans, God raised him from the dead, and that he is the world's Redeemer.

Today, many orthodox New Testament scholars provide excellent resources for credible study of the history of Jesus. In this and the following chapter we will tap into the work of Luke Timothy Johnson, emeritus professor of New Testament at Candler School of Theology, Emory University;[1] N. T. Wright, chair of New Testament and early Christianity at the School of Divinity at the University of St. Andrews;[2] and Helen K.

---

1. Luke Timothy Johnson, *The Real Jesus: The Misguided Quest for the Historical Jesus and the Truth of the Traditional Gospels* (San Francisco: HarperSanFrancisco, 1996).

2. N. T. Wright, *The Challenge of Jesus: Rediscovering Who Jesus Was and Is* (Downers Grove, IL: InterVarsity Press, 1999).

Bond, professor of Christian origins and head of the School of Divinity at the University of Edinburgh, Scotland.[3]

Wright provides reasons for studying the history of Jesus. Johnson articulates the basis for and credibility of Christian faith. Bond stresses the importance of Jesus's life as the primary pattern for Christian discipleship.

# Why Study the History of Jesus?

*First*, investigating the historical Jesus is a requisite aspect of Christian discipleship.[4] Disciplines of prayer and Bible study not rooted in Jesus can become idolatrous or self-serving.[5] Unless discipleship is grounded in discernible happenings in first-century Palestine, we are as well off to be Buddhists or Marxists or anything else.[6] If the Jesus of the Gospels is distinctly different from the one about whom Christians sing and proclaim in worship, "We are indeed living in a cloud—cuckoo-land."[7]

*Telling the story* of Jesus well is only part of our task. Christians must remember they are part of the community commissioned to model Jesus's story to the world.[8]

*Second*, Christians must embrace the imperative of truth.[9] History done well will correct faulty versions of Christianity. At the same time, it will sustain and regenerate a deep, true, surprising, and challenging orthodoxy.[10]

*Third*, we examine Jesus's history because careful study is part of the "sharp edge of our exploration into God himself."[11]

---

3. Helen K. Bond, *The Historical Jesus: A Guide for the Perplexed* (New York: T. and T. Clark, 2012). Bond cautions that the path of the Quest has not been as "tidy" as the classification indicates (7).

4. N. T. Wright, *The Challenge of Jesus*, 14.

5. Ibid., 11.

6. Ibid., 14.

7. Ibid., 18.

8. Ibid., 32.

9. Ibid., 17.

10. Ibid., 16.

11. Ibid., 14.

*Fourth*, we engage in the hard work of history to restate afresh what we believe about Jesus, the cross, the resurrection, and the incarnation.[12] Studying the life of Jesus teaches Christians the importance and meaning of modeling their lives after him.[13]

*Fifth*, because of our loyalty to the Scriptures, we take history seriously. The church is never released from the need to study Scripture anew in light of the best information we have about its world and context.[14] By using our best tools we will discover "rich, full-blooded orthodoxy bubbling up from the pages of history." The church will gain a richer vision of Jesus and of his Heavenly Father.[15]

*Sixth*, carefully engaging in the historical task helps equip the church for its mission to the world.[16]

Overall, we hope to learn: (1) Jesus's place in the Jewish world of his day; (2) Jesus's beliefs regarding the kingdom of God; (3) why Jesus died; and (4) what happened at Easter to give birth to the church.

New Testament scholar and theologian Richard Bauckham registers a caution. As helpful as historical study can be in aiding our understanding of Jesus, it can never "provide the kind of access to the reality of Jesus that Christian faith and theology have always trusted" by relying upon the Gospels.[17]

## Quests for the Historical Jesus[18]

The quest for the historical Jesus opened with the beginning of modern historical critical study of the New Testament. Richard Bauckham observes that as the twenty-first century opened, the quest for the histor-

---

12. Ibid., 17.
13. Bond, *The Historical Jesus*, 2.
14. N. T. Wright, *The Challenge of Jesus*, 17.
15. Ibid., 32.
16. Ibid., 31.
17. Richard Bauckham, *Jesus and the Eyewitnesses: The Gospels as Eyewitness Testimony*, 2nd ed. (Grand Rapids: Eerdmans, 2017), 4.
18. For a thorough treatment of the iterations of the "quest for the historical Jesus," see N. T. Wright, *Jesus and the Victory of God* (Minneapolis: Fortress Press, 1996), 3-62. For a Jewish account of the historical Jesus, see Martin Buber, *On Judaism* (New York: Schocken Books, 1967), 122-25.

ical Jesus flourished as never before.[19] There have been a series of three "quests" for the historical Jesus (four if we count the period of "no quest" after the first quest).

## The First Quest (the Old Quest)

The first quest for the historical Jesus began with German Enlightenment philosopher Hermann Samuel Reimarus (1694—1768). The "Jesus" he "discovered" satisfied Enlightenment interest in reason and a suspicion of revelation. According to Reimarus, Jesus knew the Jews were groaning under the Roman yoke and longed for a worldly deliverer.[20] So Jesus "roused the Jews" to expect speedy deliverance.[21] He would release them from bondage and establish "a wondrously glorious kingdom."[22] Jesus preached that the kingdom of heaven was at hand[23] and chose messengers who also expected a Messiah. Jesus would crush the Romans and establish God's kingdom.[24]

Jesus knew if people believed his messengers, they would accept him as the long-expected King.[25] He should have delivered the ignorant from their "coarse illusion." He did not. When it dawned on Jesus that his venture would cost his life, "he began to quiver and quake."[26] He died an abject failure, believing God had abandoned him.

What happened after Jesus's death? His mistaken and deceived disciples, their hopes crushed, "invented" a new story about a suffering spiritual Savior.[27] The Christian faith, Reimarus insisted, is built upon a "failed Messiah and a fraudulent gospel," not upon the *real* failed Jesus of Nazareth.[28]

---

19. Bauckham, *Jesus and the Eyewitnesses*, 1.

20. Hermann Samuel Reimarus, *Fragments from Reimarus*, Vol. 1 (London and Edinburgh: Williams and Northgate, 1879), trans. G. E. Lessing; ed. Charles Voysey, 12. Internet Archive. https://archive.org/details/fragmentsfromrei00reim/page/n3.

21. Ibid.

22. Ibid., 10.

23. Ibid.

24. Ibid., 11.

25. Ibid., 10.

26. Ibid., 27.

27. Ibid., 28.

28. N. T. Wright, *Jesus and the Victory of God*, 17.

This, Reimarus concluded, is the true "history of Jesus." It increasingly enlightens us.[29] N. T. Wright says Reimarus believed the Gospel writers and the early church "hushed up" the truth in order to advance their new religion.[30]

So began the quest for the "real historical Jesus" to replace the "unhistorical" Jesus of the Gospels. Some leading voices in the first quest were David Friedrich Straus (1808-74), Bruno Bauer (1809-92), Ernest Renan (1823-82), and William Wrede (1859—1906). Each believed historical study would yield a Jesus not supportive of historic Christian faith. The Gospels contain little more than the misinformed interests and beliefs of the early church. They are not much more than theological fiction.[31]

The *first* quest lasted from Reimarus until Albert Schweitzer (1875—1965), who in his *Quest of the Historical Jesus* (English edition 1910) demolished the *first quest* portraits by showing how they failed to see Jesus as an apocalyptic Jewish prophet. Attempting to place Jesus in his first-century context, Schweitzer said Jesus expected God to intervene and bring the world to an end during his ministry (Schweitzer misunderstood Jewish apocalyptic).[32]

The Jesus the *first quest* produced, Schweitzer said, never existed. Reimarus and the other questers had delivered a Jesus "designed by rationalism, endowed with life by liberalism, and clothed by modern theology in an historical garb."[33] The real historical Jesus, Schweitzer insisted, will not submit to "popular historical treatment." He cannot be made "universally intelligible to the multitude."[34] The real Jesus is for our day "a stranger and

---

29. Reimarus, *Fragments from Reimarus*, 28.

30. N. T. Wright, *Jesus and the Victory of God*, 17.

31. Reimarus, *Fragments from Reimarus*, 28.

32. N. T. Wright explains that the "end of the world picture" painted by Schweitzer "bore no relation to what actual first-century Jews believed." The new kingdom many Jews expected would "consist of a new state of affairs on earth, not the abolition of earth and its replacement with something completely different. . . . We have no evidence of people thinking the world itself would end" (N. T. Wright, *History and Eschatology*, 58). For a penetrating analysis of Schweitzer's social and philosophical "location" see N. T. Wright, *History and Eschatology*, 51-60.

33. Albert Schweitzer, *The Quest of the Historical Jesus: A Critical Study of its Progress from Reimarus to Wrede*, trans. W. Montgomery, 2nd ed. (London: Adam and Charles Black, 1911), 554. Project Gutenberg, https://www.gutenberg.org/files/45422/45422-pdf.pdf.

34. Ibid., 555.

an enigma."[35] He "overthrows the modern Jesus" Reimarus and others tailored for their Enlightenment advocates.[36] Schweitzer concluded:

> [Jesus] comes to us as One unknown, without a name, as of old, by the lake-side. He came to those men who knew Him not. He speaks to us the same word: "Follow thou me!" and sets us to the tasks which He has to fulfil for our time. He commands. And to those who obey Him, whether they be wise or simple, He will reveal Himself in the toils, the conflicts, the sufferings which they shall pass through in His fellowship, and, as an in-effable mystery, they shall learn in their own experience Who He is.[37]

The period of the first quest was followed by a period of **no quest.**

## The Second Quest (New Quest)

The *second* quest, known as "the new quest for the historical Jesus," began in 1953 with a lecture by German New Testament scholar Ernst Käsemann (1906-88), "The Promise of the Historical Jesus." Two of the major contributors were Günther Bornkamm (1905-90) and Edward Schillebeekx (1914—2009). The results of this quest were not very rewarding.[38] It never managed to develop a serious historical nerve.[39] Its portrait of Jesus "often looked far more like a twentieth-century Jewish existential philosopher than a first-century Jewish Messiah."[40]

## The Jesus Seminar

The widely known Jesus Seminar does not represent an independent "quest." It was largely a renewal of the first quest.[41] The seminar was

---

35. Ibid.
36. Ibid., 560.
37. Ibid., 561.
38. N. T. Wright, *Jesus and the Victory of God*, 24.
39. N. T. Wright, *The Challenge of Jesus*, 29.
40. N. T. Wright and Bird, *The New Testament in Its World*, 181.
41. The Jesus Seminar convened twice a year to debate the historical Jesus. It was founded in 1985 by Robert Funk (1926—2005), American biblical scholar. Funk established the Westar Institute, Santa Rosa, California, under whose auspices the Jesus Seminar convened. The seminar was co-chaired by John Dominic Crossan of DePaul University, Chicago. Though never formally disbanded, the seminar ceased functioning as the Jesus Seminar in 2006. The stated goal was to "renew the quest of the historical Jesus and to report the results of its research to the general public, rather than just to a handful of gospel specialists." Initially, the goal of the

co-founded in 1985 by American biblical scholars Robert Funk (1926—2005) and John Dominic Crossan (b. 1934), a former Roman Catholic priest. It consisted of a self-selected association of academics who convened twice a year to debate the historical Jesus. Members were committed to fact and history, honesty and candor, truth and its consequences, and science rather than superstition.[42] They generally rejected traditional views of Jesus's life and ministry and hoped to make their findings widely available.

On the basis of some recent books, N. T. Wright notes we have repeatedly been informed that the Jesus of the Gospels is historically unreliable, and Christianity is the result of error.[43] We are told that Jesus was a New Age guru, a peasant cynic, an Egyptian freemason, or a hippie revolutionary.[44]

Richard Hays levels harsh judgment against the Jesus Seminar. Its "operative methodology [was] seriously flawed." As a result, the seminar "inevitably produce[d] a skewed portrait of Jesus' teachings." Its findings "represent[ed] the idiosyncratic opinions of one particular faction of critical scholars."[45] Jesus Seminar participants practiced "entrepreneurial criticism."[46]

In the work of Bart Ehrman, professor of New Testament and early Christianity at the University of North Carolina (Chapel Hill), the spirit of the Jesus Seminar lives on. Ehrman, a former evangelical Christian, now an agnostic, is an articulate, prolific, and prominent scholar. His views are regularly sought by major media. In *How Jesus Became God: The Exaltation of a Jewish Preacher from Galilee*, Ehrman identifies Jesus as a "lower class Jewish preacher from the backwaters of rural Galilee who was condemned for illegal activities and crucified for crimes against the state." Long after Jesus's death, his followers began to claim that he was a

seminar was to review each of the sayings and deeds attributed to Jesus in the Gospels and determine which of them could be considered authentic" ("The Jesus Seminar," Westar Institute. https://www.westarinstitute.org/projects/the-jesus-seminar/). For a more detailed discussion of the Jesus Seminar, see Luke Timothy Johnson, *The Real Jesus*, 1-20.

42. N. T. Wright, *Jesus and the Victory of God*, 31.
43. N. T. Wright, *The Challenge of Jesus*, 18.
44. Ibid., 14.
45. Hays, *Reading with the Grain of Scripture*, 91.
46. Ibid., 89.

divine being. Eventually they went even further and began declaring that he was God, Lord of heaven and earth.[47]

## The Third Quest

A *third quest* began in the 1980s with the work of a growing body of scholars who differ in background and outlook. It offers rich benefits for Christian faith. N. T. Wright, whose *The Challenge of Jesus* we will examine in the next chapter, is a major voice. Others include George B. Caird, James H. Charlesworth, E. P. Sanders, and Ben Witherington.[48] They believe the history of Jesus is critical for Christian faith. So they proceed by credible historical method—hypothesis (ruthlessly tested against the evidence) and verification—a process that may yield coherent narratives.[49] Their work provides a backdrop "against which the great light of the gospel shines more brightly."[50]

Contributors to the third quest stand in the lineage of Albert Schweitzer. They take seriously the "Jewishness" of Jesus, rely heavily on first-century sources such as Qumran and Jewish apocalyptic writings, and wrestle with the complexity of the Judaism of Jesus's era. Jesus's message is evaluated not for its timeless significance but for the meaning it must have had for Jesus's audience. His crucifixion is closely examined. What must Jesus have been saying and doing beforehand to end up on a Roman cross?[51] These "questers" see Jesus as a comprehensible and yet "crucifiable" first-century Jew.[52] He must be credibly placed within his historical context.[53] One goal is to provide energy for the church's mission to the

---

47. Bart D. Ehrman, *How Jesus Became God: The Exaltation of a Jewish Preacher from Galilee* (New York: HarperOne, 2014), 1.

48. Pope Benedict XVI is not normally included. But his *Jesus of Nazareth* (Image, 2007) is strongly recommended.

49. This doesn't mean these scholars were neutral in their study of Jesus. They recognize the evidence might not fit their original assumptions, and they allow their sources to tell them things they had not expected.

50. N. T. Wright, *Jesus and the Victory of God*, 85.

51. Ibid.

52. Ibid., 86.

53. Ibid., 89.

world. Contributors believe Christians are commissioned as God's people for the world. The church must take seriously the full historical task.[54]

"Third quest" participants do not intend to replace the Spirit's role by "historical proof." They know that only through the Holy Spirit can we fully comprehend the cross of the crucified Messiah. The cross is the clearest window for peering into the heart and character of God. The "more we learn about the cross in all its historical and theological dimensions, the more we discover . . . our vocation to be the cross-bearing people, the people in whose lives and service the living God is made known."[55]

## The Basis for Christian Faith

Many scholars believe Jesus must be historically reconstructed to satisfy their Enlightenment criteria before Christian faith can be judged defensible. Luke Johnson says those requirements are "mischievous."[56] "The most destructive result is that it perpetuates the notion that Christian faith rises or falls upon verifiable historical accounts."[57] The truth is that though historical claims regarding Jesus have always been important, Christian faith has never been founded upon a historical reconstruction of Jesus. Rather, Christian faith fundamentally rests upon an affirmation regarding the present living and transforming power of Jesus.[58]

N. T. Wright agrees that historical argument alone cannot compel a person to believe Jesus was raised from the dead.[59] But "historical argument is remarkably good at clearing away the undergrowth behind which skepticisms of various sorts have long been hiding." Historical research contains "unrivaled power to explain the historical data at the heart of early Christianity."[60]

---

54. N.T. Wright, *The Challenge of Jesus*, 31.
55. Ibid., 94-95. In spite of lasting third quest contributions, N. T. Wright says that in the early decades of the twenty-first century, the third quest appears to have run its course (*The New Testament in Its World*, 183).
56. L. T. Johnson, *The Real Jesus*, 141.
57. Ibid.
58. Ibid., 133-34.
59. N. T. Wright, *Surprised by Hope* (New York: HarperOne, 2008), 64.
60. Ibid.

The Gospels and Epistles were written *primarily* as witnesses to and interpretations of Jesus's resurrection. Their "truth" is "more" than historical; they are "religiously true" because they occur in the power of the risen and present Christ, whom death failed to confine to the grave. Resurrection faith "knows" that in the deeds of Jesus of Nazareth we encounter the incarnate God. The risen Christ in his church confirms that the Father, in his Son, through the Spirit's power, successfully inaugurated his kingdom on earth.[61] The apostle Paul says the Holy Spirit pours God's love into believers, a love that births and authenticates Easter faith, and saturates and energizes discipleship and mission (Rom. 5:5).

Luke Johnson lacerates the arrogance of historians who believe the "real" must be reduced to or equated with the "historical." He accuses them of "denying any reality beyond the critic's control."[62] That, he says, "is not good history. It is instead an ideological commitment to a view of the world that insists on material explanation as the only reasonable explanation." It reduces everything to a flat plane where not even genius, much less the divine, can be considered. This view "begins with the assumption that Christianity *cannot* have anything distinctive about it."[63] By contrast, responsible historians recognize "forces and realities beyond the ken of strict historical method." They will not dismiss reality that lies beyond what historical reconstruction can demonstrate.[64]

The Nicene Creed (AD 325) contains numerous historical assertions. However, it is not true that for faith to be credible, events that gave rise to faith must first be historically verifiable.[65] Why not? *First*, by their very nature, historical reconstructions are fragile and in constant need of revision. To illustrate, the attempted Jesus reconstructions in recent years reveal "a bewildering variety of conflicting portraits of Jesus, and a distressing carelessness in the manner of arriving at those portraits."[66] They border on the humorous. *Second*, Christian faith "is simply not directed

---

61. L. T. Johnson, *The Real Jesus*, 144-45.
62. Ibid., 140.
63. Ibid.
64. Ibid.
65. Ibid., 141.
66. Ibid.

[toward] those historical facts about Jesus, or a historical reconstruction of him."[67] The New Testament clearly directs Christian faith to a living person, the resurrected Jesus whom "God has made . . . both Lord and Christ" (Acts 2:36), manifested through the powerful work of the Holy Spirit (v. 33; Rom. 1:3).

The Danish Christian Søren Kierkegaard insisted that the *real Jesus* is not a figure locked into the past, but a risen, present, contemporary Christ, reigning as Lord of all. Being a Christian means

> to become contemporary with Christ. And if becoming a Christian does not come to mean this, then all the talk about becoming a Christian is nonsense and self-deception and conceit . . . and sin against the Holy Ghost. . . . In relation to the absolute there is only one tense: the present. . . . And as Christ is the absolute, it is easy to see that with respect to Him there is only one situation: that of contemporaneousness. The five, the seven, the fifteen, the eighteen hundred years are neither here nor there; they do not change Him, neither do they in any wise *reveal* [italics mine] who He was, for who He is, is revealed only to faith.[68]

As noted earlier, Karl Barth reminds us that *revelation* of who Jesus is happens in the *event* of transformation. Johnson agrees.

> It is Jesus as risen Lord who is experienced in the assembly of believers, declared by the word of proclamation, encountered in the sacramental meal, addressed by prayers of praise and petition. It is "in the name" of *this* Jesus that the powerful deeds of healing are performed. It is through the Spirit given by this glorious Lord that believers are to express gifts of tongues and prophecy and teaching and service within the community and by the Spirit of freedom given by this Lord that they are themselves being transformed from glory to glory. So it was at the birth of the Christian faith, and so is it today wherever Christianity is spiritually alive and identifiably Christian in character.[69]

---

67. Ibid.
68. Kierkegaard, *Training in Christianity*, 409.
69. L. T. Johnson, *The Real Jesus*, 142.

The Gospels and Epistles leave no doubt about an essential continuity between Jesus the historical figure and Christ the living Lord (Phil. 2:5-11; Heb. 3:14, 18; 1 John 1:1-4). The Gospels provide access to the "real Jesus" because they bear faithful witness to him through the Spirit's power. When answering the Jewish authorities in Jerusalem who demanded they keep silent, Peter and John responded, "We cannot but speak of what we have seen and heard" (Acts 4:20, RSV).

Luke Johnson borrows an analogy from Roman Catholic theologian Karl Rahner. Christian memory of Jesus is not like that of a long-ago deceased loved one who "lives" only in our memory. No, Christian "memory" is like that of a loved one who lives with those he loves. The relationship is constantly expanding and maturing.[70]

When in the Eucharist, Christians "remember" the death and resurrection of Jesus they are not summoning the memory of some long-dead relative. The Greek word for "recalling," "remembrance," and "memory" is *anamnesis* (Luke 22:19; 1 Cor. 11:24-25). When used with reference to Jesus, Christians mean that by the Spirit, the crucified and risen Lord is "made present." This is true of the Eucharist (thanksgiving). The Eucharist "is a recollection of the past that enlivens and empowers the present as well."[71] The Christ whom the first Christians "remembered" was present to them in power. With Jesus, in the Spirit's power, they stood on the other side of the resurrection experience.[72]

Just as it was true for the first Christians, so does it happen again and again, foremost in Christian worship. Through the Holy Spirit, the risen Christ *comes* in all his fullness to meet with his people in the breaking of his body and the shedding of his blood.

---

70. Ibid., 143. Johnson is borrowing from Rahner's "On the Development of Doctrine" published in *Marquette University Journal*, Vol. 30, Issue 2, 2018.

71. For a Jew, in the Passover meal "sacred history is repeated." In the Passover ritual, "every Jew, insofar as he participates in it existentially, becomes an Israelite contemporary with Moses, whom God is drawing out of Egypt" (Herberg, *Judaism and Modern Man*, 288-89).

72. L. T. Johnson, *Writings of the New Testament*, 111-13.

# The Credibility of Christian Faith

The "good news" of the gospel of Jesus Christ has always been and always will be "a stumbling block [scandal] to Jews and folly to the Gentiles" (1 Cor. 1:23, RSV; cf. Matt. 11:25-30). "Has not God made foolish the wisdom of the world? For since, in the wisdom of God, the world did not know God through wisdom." Instead, "it pleased God through the folly of what we preach to save those who believe" (1 Cor. 1:20-21, RSV). The church must never attempt to improve on the apostle Paul: "The word of the cross is folly to these who are perishing, but to us who are being saved it is the power of God" (v. 18, RSV). To borrow from Kierkegaard, trying to construct a "gospel" void of the cross is to "sin against the Holy Ghost."[73] Not only is trying to "prove" the risen Christ by rational appeals and argument inadequate, but it is a failure to trust in the irreplaceable convincing activity of the Holy Spirit.

Finally, Luke Johnson is correct. "Proving" that Jesus is who the New Testament claims and the primary Christian creeds confess must occur in the quality of life those who make the confessions demonstrate.[74]

---

73. Kierkegaard, *Training in Christianity*, 409.
74. L. T. Johnson, *The Real Jesus*, 168.

# 11
# WHAT'S "HISTORICAL" ABOUT JESUS? (Part 2)

Is the history of Jesus important for Christian faith? *Yes*!

Can we maintain the centrality of Easter faith while examining Jesus's history? *Yes*!

*The Challenge of Jesus: Rediscovering Who Jesus Was and Is* by N. T. Wright is a good source for answering these questions. Wright identifies five important "challenges," and explains how they were met.

By examining each of these we will learn where Jesus belongs in the Jewish world of his day, what Jesus thought the kingdom of God was all about, why he died, and how Easter gave birth to the church.

## The Challenge of the Kingdom

Jesus proclaimed the kingdom of God was at hand (Mark 1:14-15; Luke 4:18-19, 43; John 18:36-38). What might the average Galilean villager have heard or expected?[1] To answer, we journey back into the world of the Old Testament as perceived and lived by first-century Jews—the world Jesus addressed.[2]

---

1. N. T. Wright, *The Challenge of Jesus*, 34.
2. Ibid.

Jesus acted on two vital convictions. *First,* he believed the creator God, from the beginning, intended to deal with human sin. Through Israel, God would redeem his world. *Second,* Jesus believed, as did many of his contemporaries, that Israel's appointed vocation would be completed as its history reached a great moment of fulfillment. Israel would be saved from its enemies and the covenant God "would at last bring his love and justice, his mercy and truth, to bear upon the whole world." This grand fulfillment would usher in universal renewal and healing.[3]

Since 587 BC, with only the intermission of the Hasmonean Dynasty (165-64 BC), first-century Palestinian Jews had lived under foreign rule. If Israel was truly God's people, why were pagans in control? Why were they oppressing God's defenseless people? Some Jews had returned from Babylonian exile. However, many believed the *theological exile* was ongoing. When would the story turn and bring the Jews out on top as promised?[4]

Most Jews longed for God's reign upon the earth.[5] God would establish justice and peace everywhere.[6] They questioned, "How and when?" There appeared to be three major options: *first,* the Qumran community that had separated from the wicked world was waiting for God to act; *second,* compromisers such as Herod and ruling Jewish elites who worked to get along with their political bosses; the *third* was offered by the Zealots. "Say your prayers, sharpen your swords, and make yourselves holy to fight a holy war." God will make you victorious over your pagan enemies. Your victory will establish good over evil.[7]

---

3. Ibid., 35. For a book-length discussion of how N. T. Wright perceived the hopes of first-century Jews, see James M. Scott, ed., *Exile: A Conversation with N. T. Wright* (Downers Grove, IL: IVP Academic, 2017). Some participants in the debate strongly support Wright's vision of first-century Judaism; others do not. A critique by Old Testament scholar Walter Brueggemann follows an introductory essay by Wright.

4. Ibid., 36.

5. Helen Bond explains that in first-century Palestine there was no consensus regarding what a Messiah and messianic age might look like. The land of Israel had known well over a century of political conflict. Stories of past glory prompted many to hope for better conditions, perhaps a gold age. Kingly and prophetic figures had arisen, but they had been quickly eliminated by Rome (*The Historical Jesus*, 66).

6. N. T. Wright, *The Challenge of Jesus*, 36-37.

7. Ibid., 37.

Jesus rejected all three options. In loving faith and prayer, he resorted to Israel's Scriptures where he found a different model. Jesus believed the kingdom of God was at hand. God was revealing his age-old plan to bring justice and mercy to Israel and the world. And he was doing it through Jesus.[8] Some of his contemporaries used vivid language to describe visions they believed to be revelatory explanations of things happening on the world scene. Often called "apocalyptic," their language—such as stars falling from the sky (Isa. 34:4)—carried theological and cosmic importance. For the most part, Jews of Jesus's day did not expect the world to end. But they did expect God to act dramatically as he had in critical moments of Israel's history.[9]

Jesus acted practically and symbolically, such as performing miracles of healing and telling parables about the kingdom of God. Perceived by the people to be a prophet, Jesus proclaimed arrival of God's kingdom in himself (Matt. 4:17; 9:35; Mark 1:13-14; Luke 4:42-44; 11:20-23). By doing so, he contested alternative kingdom dreams. Jesus's message had three central thrusts: end of exile, call of a renewed people, and warning of disaster and vindication to come.

## End of Exile

Jesus used parables such as the parable of the sower (Mark 4:1-20) and the prodigal son (Luke 15:11-32) to speak of return from exile. The *first* addresses sowing and reaping after the exile. The *second* is about exile and restoration. In and through Jesus's ministry the long-awaited moment had arrived. Exile was ending. Israel's God was establishing his kingdom in Jesus. This was *good news* (*euangelion*). Matthew and Luke tell how YAHWEH returns to his people, how in the Messiah, God fulfills all his ancient promises. The story of God's people is being "recapitulated" in Jesus's own person.[10]

---

8. Ibid.
9. Ibid., 38.
10. Ibid., 41.

## Call of a Renewed People

Jesus called forth a renewed people of God, a new world order. His stories functioned as dramatic plays where the audience is invited to audition for parts.[11] Jesus told hearers to abandon their agendas and embrace his way of being Israel. Forsake your dreams of nationalist revolution. Militarism was incompatible with Israel's vocation to become the light to the world.[12]

Jesus was offering an "utterly risky way of being Israel, the way of turning the other cheek and going the second mile, the way of losing your life to gain it."[13] He invited hearers to take up the cross, follow him, and embrace his vocation.[14] Though it angered his opponents, Jesus welcomed one and all, including the most disreputable.

As a prophet of the kingdom, Jesus seemed to show up when there were celebrations, including feasting with tax collectors and sinners (Matt. 9:9-13; Mark 2:13-17; Luke 5:27-33). Festive events were central to his message; they announced God's radical acceptance and forgiveness. This "new way" would be the "kingdom way."[15] Jesus's "renewed people" would be the vanguard of a radical turn in the life of the non-Jewish nations as well. Benefits of the "end of exile" would extend to the whole world.[16]

## Warning of Disaster and Vindication to Come

Jesus announced God's judgment would overtake Israel, not the surrounding nations, if it failed to receive its Messiah and his way of being Israel[17] and if it failed to follow the way of peace.[18] Jesus's warnings reach their peak as he rides into Jerusalem on a donkey (Matt. 21:1-11; Mark 11:1-10; Luke 19:28-44; John 12:12-15). He bursts into tears:

---

11. Ibid., 43.
12. Ibid., 44.
13. Ibid.
14. Ibid., 47.
15. Ibid., 46.
16. Ibid., 47.
17. Ibid., 49.
18. Ibid., 50.

If you, even you, had only known on this day what would bring you peace—but now it is hidden from your eyes. The days will come upon you when your enemies will build an embankment against you and encircle you and hem you in on every side. They will dash you to the ground, you and the children within your walls. They will not leave one stone on another, because you did not recognize the time of God's coming to you. (Luke 19:41-44, NIV)

## The Challenge of the Symbols

Why was Jesus killed? Because he attacked what had become central Jewish symbols in the Second Temple Jewish world (c. 516 BC to AD 70).[19] The kingdom was arriving on earth as in heaven. A new day was dawning. Symbols needed to be reconfigured.

The key symbols of Judaism were Sabbath, food, nation and land, and temple.

### Sabbath

The Pharisees monitored Sabbath observance. The Sabbath prefigured the messianic age to come. Jesus repeatedly angered the Pharisees by acting with sovereign freedom. Contrary to what they permitted, Jesus healed on the Sabbath and followed up by declaring, "The Son of Man is lord of the Sabbath" (Matt. 12:8; see vv. 1-8; Mark 2:23-27; Luke 6:1-11). Because the Sabbath signaled release from bondage and captivity, it was the most appropriate day for healing. Jesus was announcing that in his ministry, Israel's long-awaited Sabbath day was dawning.[20]

Jesus was not dismissive of the Sabbath. He customarily observed the Sabbath (Luke 4:14-15).

### Food

The purity codes, especially the dietary rules enforced by the Pharisees, constituted a pivotal symbol that distinguished Israel from its impure pagan neighbors. In numerous instances Jesus violated the purity codes, including eating with sinners (Mark 2:13-17; Luke 5:27-32). He redefined

19. Ibid., 55.
20. Ibid., 60.

purity as based upon "inwardness," upon the "heart," not upon food restrictions that distinguished between pure Jews and sinful Gentiles. On one occasion Jesus said, "Listen to me, all of you, and understand: there is nothing outside a person that by going in can defile, but the things that come out are what defile" (Mark 7:14-15). On that occasion Jesus declared all foods clean (v. 19).

To be sure, Jesus was not dismissive of purity. He takes purity very seriously, but he redefines and overcomes it.

## Nation and Land

Family and national identity mattered supremely to the Pharisees. Family members were supposed to evidence solidarity with each other. They were supposed to pursue goals that increased the family's well-being and social status.[21] To challenge family was to challenge national identity—Israel's common descent from Abraham.

Some of Jesus's most stunning statements appeared to undermine family. "Let the dead bury their own dead, but as for you, go and proclaim the kingdom of God" (Luke 9:60). In Jesus's culture, burying one's father took precedence even over saying the Shema (Deut. 6:4). Jesus countered that announcing the kingdom is more important. "I have come," he said, "to turn a man against his father, a daughter against her mother" (Matt. 10:35, NIV). To inherit the age to come one must take leave of traditional familial and national identity.[22]

Jesus saw restoration of broken and damaged people as the restoration of land.[23] The arriving kingdom introduced healing and blessing. Healings symbolized new creation. The lame, the deaf, and the dumb were not to be excluded from community. Their healing signaled Jesus's *reconstitution of Israel*.[24] He was creating a new family, formed around himself, with a new identity (Mark 3:34-35). The new community would embody God's kingdom.[25]

---

21. N. T. Wright and Bird, *The New Testament in Its World*, 113.
22. N. T. Wright, *The Challenge of Jesus*, 60-61.
23. Ibid., 68.
24. Ibid.
25. Ibid., 69.

## Temple

For most Jews, the temple was the center of Judaism. Here heaven and earth overlapped. Here sacrifices were offered, sins were forgiven, and the relationship between God and Israel was regularly renewed. It was "the place where the union and fellowship between Israel and her God was endlessly and tirelessly consummated."[26] In Jesus's day, Jews believed the temple was the location from which divine powers spread to the whole world. It "sanctified" the city of Jerusalem and the land of Israel.[27] The temple also carried many royal overtones: David, Solomon, Hezekiah, and Josiah (Wright notes that "temple and messiahship went hand in hand").[28]

The first two chapters of Luke feature the temple's importance in Jesus's life. At the time of purification according to the law of Moses (Lev. 12:2-8), Joseph and Mary "brought [Jesus] up to Jerusalem to present him to the Lord" (Luke 2:22; see vv. 22-24). While they were there, Simeon recognized in the child Jesus "a light for revelation to the gentiles and for glory to your people Israel" (v. 32). Jesus recognized the unique role of priests in declaring lepers clean and hence ready to reenter society (Luke 5:12-16). Much of the action in the first half of John's Gospel happens in or near the temple. John liberally employs imagery involving feasts associated with temple rites.

YAHWEH had dwelt in the temple until the Babylonians destroyed it and took Israel into exile (587/6 BC; 2 Kings 25:8-12; Jer. 52:12-23). He would do so again. Ezekiel graphically describes YAHWEH abandoning the temple (Ezek. 10:1-22; 11:22-25). But the abandonment would not be permanent. Someday YAHWEH would return in glory (Ezek. 43:1-12; cf. Mal. 3:1). In Jesus's day, the glorious return had not happened. There is no record in Second Temple Judaism of that having occurred. Israel waited.

---

26. Ibid., 63.

27. Lawrence H. Schiffman, "The Second Temple," Bible Odyssey. https://www.bible odyssey.org/places/main-articles/second-temple. John Walton says that in the ancient Near East a temple was "considered the center of power, control, and order from which deity brings order to the human world. Fertility, prosperity, peace, and justice emanate from his presence there" (*Ancient Near Eastern Thought and the Old Testament*, 127).

28. N. T. Wright, *The Challenge of Jesus*, 63.

Jesus acted and spoke as if he were supposed to replace what the temple did and was. He forgave sins with no prior requirement for temple worship or sacrifice (Luke 5:17-26; 7:36-50; 23:39-43). This was equivalent to someone offering as a private person to issue someone else a passport or a driver's license.[29] In Matthew the angel of the Lord told Joseph this would happen. Mary's child would be named "Jesus [*Joshua*, "YAHWEH saves" or "YAHWEH is salvation"], for he will save his people from their sins" (Matt. 1:21). John announces that God's glory [Gr. *doxa*; Heb. *kâbôd*] was revealed in the Word who "became flesh and dwelt [tabernacled] among us, full of grace and truth" (John 1:13-14, RSV; cf. Heb. 1:3).

*In Jesus,* YAHWEH *had returned to the temple as promised.* He is the new temple. In him the Creator and Redeemer now dwell. In him the Father is being revealed.[30] Completely anchored in first-century Judaism, Jesus was reconstituting the people of God.

Isaiah, Jeremiah, Ezra, Nehemiah, and Daniel had explained that Israel's exile in Babylon was caused by its sins, especially its habitual idolatry. Exile would end when God finally forgave Israel's sins. If sin that caused exile has been forgiven, as Jesus was doing, then exile is over. The long-awaited reign of God in the person of Jesus has begun.[31]

## The Challenge of a Crucified Messiah

Did Jesus think of himself as Messiah? Did he see himself as the embodiment of Israel's God? Wright says the Gospels answer "yes." Jesus was a "thinking, reflective theologian."[32] Historians must pay attention to Jesus's own self-awareness.[33]

Messianic expectations in Israel included hope for liberation, the end of exile, defeat of evil, and return of YAHWEH to the temple. The Messiah would: (1) build or restore the temple, and (2) fight the decisive battle

---

29. Ibid., 65.
30. N. T. Wright, *History and Eschatology*, 182.
31. N. T. Wright, *The Challenge of Jesus*, 73.
32. Ibid., 75.
33. Ibid.

against the enemy. He would "rescue Israel and bring God's justice to the world."[34]

Jesus did none of this as Jews had expected.

The title on Jesus's cross—"Jesus of Nazareth, the King [*basileus*] of the Jews" (John 19:19)—indicated he was crucified as a would-be Messiah. His gruesome death certainly seemed to prove otherwise. Nevertheless, belief that Jesus is the true Messiah is deeply rooted in early Christianity. By the time Paul used the term *Christos* ("anointed one"; Gr. for "Messiah") it was already fixed to Jesus's name: Jesus Christ, or Jesus *the* Christ. His resurrection confirmed for his followers that the title was correct.

But before Jesus's crucifixion and resurrection there had been evidence of Jesus being Israel's Messiah. His triumphal entry into Jerusalem on Palm Sunday and his disruptive action in the temple (Matt. 21:12-13; Mark 11:15-19; Luke 19:45-46; John 2:13-22) are events that contain royal overtones.

*Palm Sunday.* Many Jews would have recalled that before Judas Maccabeus (d. 160 BC, son of the priest Mattathias who initiated a successful revolt against Antiochus IV Epiphanes) purified the temple, he entered Jerusalem waving palm fronds (2 Macc. 10:7). This symbolized "royal" Jewish victory over pagan domination.

*Temple action.* By what authority did Jesus disrupt and close the temple for much of a day? He was the King acting on God's behalf. If we begin with Jesus's temple action and work outward, we discover numerous instances in Jesus's ministry that explain and confirm his "royal" action in the temple. N. T. Wright calls them "royal riddles."[35] They have "a natural home within the proclamation of Jesus himself."[36] Some of them are:

- At Jesus's baptism, the Father confirms Jesus's messianic identity and mission (Mark 1:9-11; cf. Matt. 2:13-17; Luke 3:21-22).
- While walking in the temple, Jesus is asked by Jewish authorities by what authority he was behaving in an apparently messianic manner. Jesus asks what they thought of John the Baptist. They refuse to

---

34. Ibid., 76.
35. Ibid., 77.
36. Ibid., 79.

answer. But Jesus cryptically implies that if John was Elijah who was to appear prior to the Messiah, then Jesus must be the Messiah (Mark 11:27-33).

- In the parable of the wicked tenants (Matt. 21:33-46; Mark 12:1-9), Jesus implies that he is the son who, though rejected by the tenants, authoritatively represents his Father's claims upon Israel.
- In Mark 12:10-11 Jesus signals that he is the "cornerstone" chosen by the Lord but rejected by the builders. Jesus is building the eschatological (final) temple.
- Speaking to the Pharisees, Jesus redefines Davidic messiahship. The Pharisees say the Messiah will be David's son. Jesus corrects them by quoting Psalm 110:1. "How is it then that David, inspired by the Spirit, calls him Lord?" (Matt. 22:43, RSV). Referring directly to himself, Jesus claims to possess authority even over King David.

The pre-Resurrection evidence upon which the early church based its identification of Jesus shows that Jesus saw himself as the Messiah from at least the time of his baptism.[37] His ministry was marked by a redefined messiahship that paralleled his entire kingdom proclamation.

## The Challenge of Jesus, and God

Jesus's Jewish contemporaries believed in a specific God of whom there was only one. He created and transcended the world, was present and active in it, and was sovereign over it. They knew him as YAHWEH, though they did not use his name for fear of misusing it (Deut. 5:11). They normally used masculine pronouns, but often used feminine imagery, realizing God was beyond gender distinctions.

This one true God had called Israel to be his special people, but not as an end in itself. Israel was chosen for the sake of the larger world. Through Israel as his messenger, God would rescue and heal the world. Israel learned its vocation through the complex story of Abraham's family, the story of *covenant*. It included descent into Egypt, slavery, exodus, land, rebellion, and exile—seeming annihilation. In many ways, especially through its

---

37. Ibid., 81.

festivals, Israel looked back upon its story to know who God is and what they hoped he would do again to reconstitute them as his people.[38]

Without ceasing to be Jewish monotheists, the earliest Christians concluded they should worship Jesus. In *Jesus and the God of Israel*, Richard Bauckham explains that "early Judaism had clear and consistent ways of characterizing the one God and, thus, distinguishing the one God absolutely from all other reality."[39] When New Testament Christology is understood with reference to the Jewish context, "it becomes clear that from the earliest post-Easter beginnings, early Christians included Jesus precisely and unambiguously within the unique identity of the one God of Israel."[40] Bauckham calls the earliest Christology "a Christology of divine identity."[41] So Jesus's resurrection confirmed in its fullness what the disciples had encountered from the beginning (e.g., Mark 1:20).

Paul includes Jesus when speaking of the one true God. Pivotal texts are 1 Corinthians 8:1-6, Philippians 2:5-11, Galatians 4:1-8, and Colossians 1:15-20. For Paul, "There is but one God, the Father, from whom all things came and for whom we live; and there is but one Lord [*Kyrios*], Jesus Christ, through whom all things came and through whom we live" (1 Cor. 8:6, NIV). This is a remarkable adaptation of the Shema (Deut. 6:4, stated above).

Paul's statement affirms that creation and redemption originate in the Father and are implemented through Christ who is God as the Father is God.[42] At this earliest stage of Christian development, Paul's affirmation captures all that the early church affirmed in its formative creeds regarding the relationship between Father and Son. After Paul's clear affirmation we must conclude that "if Trinitarian theology had not existed it would be necessary to invent it."[43] Remarkably, on the basis of God's full revelation of himself in the Spirit-sending Son, Wright concludes Paul

38. Ibid.
39. Richard Bauckham, *Jesus and the God of Israel* (Grand Rapids: Eerdmans, 2008), ix.
40. Ibid.
41. Ibid., x.
42. N. T. Wright, *The Challenge of Jesus*, 107.
43. Ibid.

found it necessary to "redefine Jewish monotheism"[44] as "Christological monotheism."[45] He, along with other early followers of Jesus, was motivated by the conviction that "the prophetic promise of YHWH's return, and the new exodus associated with it, had transpired in Jesus' person and work."[46] Supremely in Jesus, Israel's God had done what he had long promised.

> He had returned to be king. He had "visited" his people and "redeemed" them. He had come back to dwell in the midst of his people. Jesus had done—in his life, death, resurrection, and ascension—what God had said he and he alone would do. He had inaugurated God's kingdom on earth as in heaven. . . . [Paul] was compelled to use Jesus-language for the one true God.[47]

Where did all this begin? Did it originate with Jesus? As noted earlier, at the center of Jesus's understanding was his belief that he was called to do and be in relation to Israel what the temple was and did. He assumed the role of the temple and legitimated his actions with Davidic claims (2 Sam. 7:12-13). He was the place and means by which God was finally present with his people. He was the Shekinah, the glorious presence, in person, YAHWEH's presence dwelling with his people.[48]

As noted earlier, a central feature of Jesus's ministry was that he forgave sins, which only God could do. He welcomed and feasted with "sinners." Israel's God was present and active in him, *the new covenant way* for which Israel had been longing. Jesus was the new exodus, the pillar of cloud and fire leading God's people to freedom. The first exodus (Exod. 13:17-22) revealed the meaning of the *name* YAHWEH (3:13-15). Jesus revealed the *person* of YAHWEH in human form (John 1:14-18; 8:58; 14:7-11; Col. 1:15-29. As the Light of the World (cf. John 8:12) he would fulfill Israel's calling.[49]

---

44. N. T. Wright, *Paul in Fresh Perspective* (Minneapolis: Fortress Press, 2005), 99.
45. N. T. Wright and Bird, *The New Testament in Its World*, 372.
46. Ibid.
47. Ibid.
48. N. T. Wright, *The Challenge of Jesus*, 114.
49. Ibid., 116.

Jesus's last great journey to Jerusalem, climaxing in his temple action and the upper room, was intended to symbolize, enact, and personify the long-awaited return of YAHWEH to Zion (Jerusalem and the temple). Wright believes Jesus intended the stories he told about a king or master returning to check on his servants (Matt. 25:14-30; Luke 19:11-27) as indicating YAHWEH coming to Jerusalem to judge and to save.[50] The stories picked up Malachi's warning: "The Lord whom you seek will suddenly come to his temple. The messenger of the covenant in whom you delight—indeed, he is coming, says the LORD of hosts. But who can endure the day of his coming, and who can stand when he appears?" (Mal. 3:1-2).

Jesus's entrance into Jerusalem on Palm Sunday was not casual. "The time of your visitation" (Luke 19:44) meant YAHWEH was returning to settle accounts and to bring all things to their appointed conclusion.[51]

The anticipated Shekinah glory had a human face (cf. 2 Cor. 4:3-6)[52] surrounded by a crown of thorns.[53] "We have seen his glory, the glory of the one and only Son, who came from the Father, full of grace and truth" (John 1:14, NIV).[54]

## The Challenge of Easter

Jesus's resurrection lies at the center of the church's faith and self-understanding (cf. Acts 4:1-2). It informs all dimension of Christian faith, including baptism, justification, ethics, and future hope.

Wright examines the rise of early Christianity from three perspectives.

*First,* early Christianity was *a kingdom of God movement.* By the time of Paul, "kingdom of God" had become a shorthand way for identifying the young Christian community. It meant God was establishing his rule in the world. When Paul affirmed "Jesus is Lord" he meant Caesar is not. This is a "no king but God" theology with Jesus in the center.

---

50. Ibid., 117.
51. Ibid., 118.
52. Ibid., 120.
53. Ibid., 124.
54. Ibid., 122.

Being a kingdom of God movement entailed the end of exile, God's return to Zion, renewal of the world, and establishment of God's justice for the cosmos. Clearly, the kingdom had not arrived as most first-century Jews expected. So why did the early church make this claim?

In 1 Corinthians 15 Paul explains the kingdom was coming in two stages. It had been inaugurated in power *and* would be consummated in future glory. In the between time, Christians were to organize their lives and act as return-from-exile people of the new covenant. This was *neither* a nationalist Jewish movement *nor* one reduced to private mystical experience.

*Second*, from the beginning, the Jesus movement was a *resurrection movement*, its central driving force. From Ezekiel 37 onward, "resurrection" denoted the great return from exile, renewal of God's covenant with his people. Israel's sin and exile had been dealt with. Resurrection was the symbol for the coming new age, the new covenant. Abraham, Isaac, and Jacob and all God's people would be raised to new life in God's new world.[55]

The new age had neither dawned as first-century Jews expected, nor had the resurrection of all God's people occurred. Yet the early church stoutly affirmed that in Jesus the resurrection of the dead had already happened (Acts 4:2). They ordered their practice, their defining stories, their symbolic world, and their theology around this fixed belief.[56] They behaved as though the new age had already arrived. In the Spirit's power they proclaimed the resurrection and its meaning to Jew and Gentile alike.

Paul told the Colossians God had already "delivered [them] from the dominion of darkness and transferred [them] to the kingdom of his beloved Son, in whom we have redemption, the forgiveness of sins" (Col. 1:13-14, RSV). Consequently, from now on, believers were to "lead a life worthy of the Lord, fully pleasing to him" (v. 10, RSV). Jesus is the "firstborn from the dead" (v. 18, RSV). Although not all the righteous dead had been raised, one *person* had been raised to new life in the middle of the present age.

55. Ibid., 135.
56. Ibid., 138.

*Third,* early Christianity was a *messianic movement.* The Gospels teach that Jesus spoke and acted as Messiah. Such claims caused his death. If that had been his end, there is no good way to explain why the early church continued to believe Jesus was the Messiah. Their worldview, beliefs, and practices were reordered around this conviction. At the risk of their lives, they traveled the eastern Mediterranean proclaiming Jesus as the *kyrios kosmou,* Lord of the world. With one voice they testified they had encountered the risen Christ and could do no other than proclaim him as the Messiah of God. "Men of Israel," Peter proclaimed on the Day of Pentecost, "Jesus of Nazareth, a man attested to you by God with mighty works and wonders and signs which God did through him . . .—this Jesus . . . you crucified and killed . . . But God raised him up, having loosed the pangs of death, because it was not possible for him to be held by it" (Acts 2:22-24, RSV).

Convergence of evidence, N. T. Wright concludes, drives us back to a great, unanticipated event in history and to Jesus the historical person. As the Father intended, Jesus embodied Israel's God. He accomplished all the Father purposed for him. "He will feed his flock like a shepherd, he will gather the lambs in his arms, he will carry them in his bosom, and gently lead those that are with young" (Isa. 40:11, RSV; cf. John 17:1-8). This is Old Testament portrayal of YAHWEH, "but it fits Jesus like a glove."[57]

## Conclusion

Jesus was fully aware of his vocation as fulfilling all that was included in the Jewish symbols of temple, Torah, Word, Spirit, and wisdom.[58] He achieved the great exodus, not only for Israel but for the whole world, through which the name and character of YAHWEH would be fully revealed.[59]

---

57. N. T. Wright and Bird, *The New Testament in Its World,* 240-41.
58. N. T. Wright, *The Challenge of Jesus,* 123.
59. Ibid., 122.

# 12
# JESUS AS THE GOSPELS PRESENT HIM

## Introduction

This chapter draws upon scholars who understand the comprehensive beauty, distinct planning, and complementarity of the Gospels. The "parts" contribute to a convergent "whole." The writers of the four Gospels planned carefully, utilized established genre, exhibited biblical acumen and interpretive ability, and drew extensively upon named eyewitness.[1] Their skillful and subtle execution shows they were anything but overheated amateurs or self-serving propagandists.

## What Is a Gospel?

"Gospel" comes from the Greek word *euangelion*, which means "good news." In the larger Greco-Roman world, "gospel" referred to the announcement of good news, such as victory in battle or the birth of a child.

---

1. Bauckham, *Jesus and the Eyewitnesses*. Jesus's teachings were transmitted not only by anonymous sources but also by "named eyewitnesses, in whose name they were transmitted and who remained the living and active guarantors of the tradition" (290). In addition to the disciples, Bauckham identifies, among others, Simon of Cyrene, Bartimaeus, Jairus, and the relatives of Jesus (xii, 297-98).

For example: the birth of Augustus in 63 BC was the beginning of "good news" for the world, a change of things for the better.

In the New Testament, "gospel" means good news about what Jesus Christ proclaimed and did, about who he is. It refers to the long-anticipated coming of God to establish his dominion over all the earth. Grounded in Old Testament anticipation, the Gospels tell how God fulfilled his promises to Israel in and through Jesus the Messiah, through his life, death, and resurrection.

Authors of the four Gospels are "Evangelists," bearers of good tidings. They narrate the life, death, and resurrection of Jesus as the "gospel of God" (Mark 1:14, RSV; see Matt. 1:1; Mark 1:1). According to them, hopes found in the Law and the Prophets have been fulfilled *in* and *by* Jesus (Matt. 1:1-23; Mark 1:1-4, 14-15; Luke 1:26-35; 24:1-12; John 1:14-18). To "believe the gospel" is to embrace the Gospels' interpretation of the person and ministry of Jesus (Mark 1:14-15).

For all four Evangelists, the story of Jesus reaches its height in his crucifixion and resurrection. They are paradoxically aware that on the cross, Jesus was enthroned as the world's rightful Lord.[2] In retrospect, after Jesus's resurrection and ascension they fully discerned in his public ministry and crucifixion the presence of Israel's God.[3] All four Evangelists declare that in Jesus's resurrection a new world—a rescued, renewed, and transformed creation—was born.

Richard Bauckham counsels us to hear the Gospels as "testimonies." As such, they are "entirely appropriate means of access to the historical reality of Jesus."[4]

## Genre

The Evangelists did not create a new kind of literature. They adapted a prominent Greco-Roman genre- biography (*bios*). In this respect, the Gospels are similar to biographies of figures such as Socrates and Julius Caesar. Unlike them, the Gospels are closely linked to the story of Israel

---

2. N. T. Wright, *History and Eschatology*, 147, 152.
3. Ibid., 144.
4. Bauckham, *Jesus and the Eyewitnesses*, 5.

and are similar to biographies of Abraham, Joseph, or Moses. More importantly, they uniquely proclaim the gospel of God, the *kerygma* (proclamation). They present Jesus as the Messiah, and his death and resurrection as part of his messianic calling. The Gospels uniformly proclaim that Jesus is the world's Redeemer. "Through the events concerning Jesus, the creator God had become king on earth as in heaven."[5]

In antiquity a biography conveyed the importance of a person's life, was written in continuous prose, developed roughly along chronological lines, and rarely focused on a person's childhood. A biography legitimated a specific view of its subject and sought to confirm its audience as "gatekeepers" of the subject's memory, character, way of life, and death.

The Gospels include additional literary forms: parables, birth narratives, genealogies, and farewell discourses. They assume readers have already begun to embrace the unconventional values proclaimed and lived by Jesus.

Until fairly recently, scholars debated the genre of the Gospels, often making distinctions between biography (Matthew, Mark, John), and history (Luke), or some mixture thereof. Today New Testament scholarship has moved to almost universal identification of the Gospels as ancient biography. According to New Testament scholar Kent Brower, considering all four Gospels as biography makes clear that the early church considered the life of Jesus important for salvation, as well as his death/resurrection/ascension/return. Jesus's life matters as a model of complete obedience to his Heavenly Father that leads to death at the hands of the Romans, and to resurrection by the power of God.[6]

## Consistency of Witness

Though possessing distinctive voices, the four Gospels are impressively consistent in their identity of Jesus and his mission. Through his story the Gospels reveal "an essential and seamless continuity between the story of Israel and the story of the Church."[7] Each Evangelist understands

---

5. N. T. Wright and Bird, *The New Testament in Its World*, 683.

6. Conversation with Kent Brower, 9/1/2022.

7. Paul J. Achtemeier, Joel B. Green, and Marianne Meye Thompson, *Introducing the New Testament: Its Literature and Theology* (Grand Rapids: Eerdmans, 2001), 53. Recent enthu-

Jesus's identity "within the framework of Israel's fierce loyalty to the one God of all the earth."[8] Each one identifies Jesus as embodying the God of Israel.[9] The characteristic focus is neither on Jesus's wondrous deeds nor on his wise words. Instead, their uniform focus is on the *character* of Jesus's life and death. All four Gospels agree regarding the meaning of discipleship. It is to follow the same messianic pattern.[10]

The diversity of the Gospel witness, says Luke Timothy Johnson, is more a gift than a problem.[11] They display a remarkable unity in how they understand Jesus. Shaped by creative minds, the Gospels offer a *"repertoire* of faithful ways to receive and proclaim God's word."[12] All "bear the impress of poets, preachers and prophets."[13] Richard Hays adds that we should hear the Gospel testimonies "as four distinct voices singing in *polyphony* (i.e., harmonizing parts)."[14] The differing portrayals of Jesus converge and cohere as distinct witnesses to the same unified story.[15] They agree in how they understand the redemptive purpose and effect of Jesus's death: an act of radical faithfulness to God's plan for Israel and the world.[16] Together they extend a clear invitation to everyone to enter

---

siasm for the Gnostic Gospels and criticism of the early church for rejecting them runs rough-shod over contents of the church's evangelical faith as criteria for embracing the four Gospels and rejecting other "candidates." The "canonizing process" was "catholic" and cautious.

8. Hays, *Echoes of Scripture*, 362. Hays says, "This is one of the features that marks the distinction between the canonical Gospels and those later extra-canonical writings that either ignore or repudiate Israel and Israel's God. The canonical Evangelists understood themselves as standing *within* the still-unfolding narrative trajectory of Israel's covenantal relationship with the God of Abraham, Isaac, and Jacob" (ibid.).

9. Ibid., 363. This doesn't deny that the Jesus of the Gospels is a human figure. On the contrary, identification of Jesus as Israel's God simultaneously portrays him as a man who hungers, suffers, and dies on a cross (ibid., 363-64).

10. Ibid.

11. L. T. Johnson, *The Real Jesus*, 147.

12. Hays, *Echoes of Scripture*, 356.

13. L. T. Johnson, *The Writings*, 461.

14. Richard B. Hays, *Reading Backwards: Figural Christology and the Fourfold Gospel Witness* (Waco, TX: Baylor University Press, 2014), 95.

15. Hays, *Reading with the Grain of Scripture*, 25.

16. Ibid., 22.

God's unfolding drama of redemption, and to pattern their lives after the story of Jesus.[17]

Luke Johnson identifies three positive implications of the fourfold Gospel diversity: (1) the presentation of Jesus is richer than could have been achieved in a single version; (2) the fourfold witness symbolizes the infinite *replicability* and *applicability* of the story of Jesus in the church and in the lives of Christians; (3) the plurality of the Gospels points to the fact that the *meaning* of Jesus is not to be found in segmented "facts" but in the *pattern* of Jesus's life as one of radical obedience to God and service to others. This pattern can be formed in the lives of Christians by the Holy Spirit. Paul calls this the "law of Christ" (Gal. 6:2), the pattern of the Messiah.[18]

The Gospels tell how the Redeemer God has come to Israel, and the whole world. They come with the authority of God. Jesus has the power to speak and act decisively, even to forgive sins (Mark 2:10). This happens often in the Synoptic Gospels (e.g., Matt. 7:29; 9:6; 28:18; Mark 1:22, 27; Luke 4:32, 36; 5:24).

For "outsiders," Jesus's death is that of a condemned criminal who could do nothing to avert his fate (John 5:18; 6:64; 7:1; 8:15). But for "insiders" Jesus's death is a willing sacrifice for the sake of others. He dies "for the nation, and not for the nation only, but to gather into one the children of God who are scattered abroad" (11:51-52, RSV). As "the good shepherd" he willingly "lays down his life for the sheep" (10:11; see vv. 7-18). He is singularly the one in whom God's love for the world is definitively manifest, so that now, anyone who receives him as Redeemer will never "perish but . . . have eternal life" (3:16).

## The Synoptic Gospels

Matthew, Mark, and Luke are Synoptic Gospels (see endnote for explanation).[19]

---

17. Ibid., 23. Hays is speaking specifically of Hebrews. But he intends the statement for the Gospels as well.

18. L. T. Johnson, *The Real Jesus*, 149.

19. The term "synoptic" refers to the shared point of view found in Matthew, Mark, and Luke. The Greek text of these Gospels is in many places so nearly identical that some form of

## Matthew

Written in the decades following the Roman destruction of Jerusalem (AD 70), the Gospel of Matthew is characterized by a skillful and highly intentional use of Scripture.[20]

According to Matthew, Jesus is Emmanuel, God with us (1:23; Isa. 7:10-17). By placing the Isaiah citation at the beginning, Matthew establishes a major theme for his Gospel. In the person of Jesus, Israel's God is present with his people, the embodied presence of God, the one to whom worship belongs (2:2, 11; 8:2; 9:18; 14:32-33; 15:25; 28:9; 28:17).[21] To worship Jesus (e.g., Matt. 28:17) is to worship YAHWEH, not merely God's agent or intermediary.[22] In Matthew 18:20 Jesus explicitly declares himself to be the Emmanuel promised in 1:23. Moreover, as God, he will always be with his people in mission and wherever they gather and invoke his name (Matt. 28:16-20).[23] As "bookends," the Emmanuel affirmations in 1:23 and 28:16-20 frame Matthew's Gospel. They prepare us to hear his presentation of Jesus as the *Gospel of God*. Throughout, the book teaches why the disciples and the early church worshipped Jesus Messiah as God (14:32-33; 28:17).

Matthew's opening sentence, "The book of the genealogy of Jesus Christ, the son of David, the son of Abraham" (1:1, RSV), serves as a title. It suggests the story of Jesus is a "new Genesis," the story of redemption that begins the world anew.[24] The Redeemer is Jesus Christ, son of David (archetypical king of Israel), and son of Abraham (Israel's patriarchal forefather). These identifications connect "new creation" with Israel's past.[25]

---

borrowing from one to another must have happened. Trying to understand why the Synoptic Gospels agree so closely in some places and disagree so widely in others is called the Synoptic (seen together) Problem. For a full discussion of the Synoptic Problem, see Dennis Bratcher, "The Gospels and The Synoptic Problem: The Literary Relationship of Matthew, Mark, and Luke," The Voice. http://www.crivoice.org/synoptic.html.

20. Hays, *Echoes of Scripture*, 157.
21. Ibid., 167.
22. Ibid., 175.
23. Ibid., 145.
24. Ibid., 110.
25. Ibid.

Throughout, Matthew shows that in Jesus's life, teachings, death, and resurrection all Scripture has been fulfilled.[26] As Israel's representative, Jesus overcomes its unfaithfulness and saves his people from their sins (1:21). Jesus Messiah is the obedient "Son of God" in a way Israel had failed to be.[27] He carries forward the story of God's unbreakable redemptive love for his people.[28] The result will be rescue of Israel as anticipated in the exodus story, now brought to completion in Jesus.[29]

The earthly Jesus is now the risen and exalted One. In his abiding presence, Jesus's story continues in and through his community that embodies radical obedience to Torah as authoritatively interpreted by Jesus (Matt. 5—7).[30] He calls believers to worship and faithful mission as they bear hopeful witness to the world. His mission entails "the end of exile, the regathering of elect Israel, and the restoration of a glorious fruit-bearing kingdom under the rule of Jesus himself."[31]

Matthew has been called "the Gospel of the Church." He alone among the Evangelists uses the term *ekklesia* (church, 16:18; 18:17; a gathering of citizens called out from their homes into some public place, an assembly). Matthew has been most often used in worship. Its contents and structure demonstrate the author's desire to provide clear and coherent guidance for a community of believers.[32]

Matthew loves system. The book's five major discourses provide a manifesto for the church (chs. 5—7; 9:36—10:42; 13:1-52; 18; 23—25). The conclusion of each discourse is marked by "When Jesus had finished saying these words." The discourses are characterized by fullness and symmetry. *First*, in them we find treated the law (5:17-48), piety (6:1-18), demands of discipleship (10:1-42), parables of the kingdom (13:1-52), relations in the church (18:1-35), polemic against opponents (23:1-39), and eschatology—fulfilment of God's kingdom (24:4—25:46). *Second*,

---

26. Ibid., 139.
27. Ibid., 140.
28. Ibid., 113.
29. Ibid., 114.
30. Ibid., 121.
31. Ibid., 138.
32. L. T. Johnson, *The Writings*, 165.

Matthew uses similar formal elements within each discourse: parables in chapter 13, beatitudes and antitheses in chapter 5, and woes in chapter 23. *Third,* he uses numerical groupings. The genealogy has three sets of fourteen generations, thereby including the number 7 in the calculation as well (1:1-17). There are three angelic messages for Joseph (1:20; 2:13, 19), three temptations of Jesus (4:1-11), three modes of piety (6:1-18), and more. Matthew uses other numerical groupings as well, such as six (the antitheses, 5:21-48), seven (parables and woes, chaps. 13 and 23), and ten (miracles, chaps. 8 and 9).[33]

Reminiscent of YAHWEH addressing Moses on a mountain, Jesus delivers a sermon on a mount (5:1—7:27). His final words are spoken on a Galilean mountain (28:16); they are *retrospective* (calling to mind all Jesus has done and commanded) and *prospective* (outlining the church's missionary and disciple-making mission). Jesus invites future followers to place themselves in the narrative. His final words frame the entire Gospel around the ongoing presence of God.

Matthew's instructions regarding discipleship agree with Mark: the path of discipleship follows the steps of the suffering Messiah (Isa. 53). Matthew expands Mark's understanding of discipleship to include persecution of the church and becoming a servant to others within the community (5:11-12; 6:44; 10:16-24; 18:5-21; 24:9-14; 25:31-66).[34]

## Mark

In some ways, this shortest Gospel is the strangest and most difficult to grasp.[35] It was written either immediately after the Romans attacked and plundered the Jerusalem temple (AD 70) or in the time of unrest leading up to that cataclysm.[36] Mark reconfigures the Jewish hope around Jesus; in him, Israel's expectations are fulfilled.

---

33. Ibid., 166-68.

34. L. T. Johnson, *The Real Jesus,* 154.

35. L. T. Johnson, *The Writings,* 143.

36. Hays, *Echoes of Scripture,* 18. For a detailed account of that event see "The Siege of Jerusalem in 70 CE," *World History Encyclopedia.* https://www.worldhistory.org/article/1993/the-siege-of-jerusalem-in-70-ce/.

We do not know for certain the author's identity or his intended audience. So far as we know, Mark was first to place the life of Jesus in narrative form. From then on, "Gospel" carried the sense of a literary medium and message. There is strong reason to believe that the apostle Peter was an important source for Mark.[37]

According to Mark, Old Testament prophecies regarding the return of the Lord to redeem his people are being fulfilled in Jesus. Mark quotes Malachi's promise of God's return (Mark 1:2; Mal. 3:1) and couples it with Isaiah shouting to Zion that its God is returning, coming in glory (Mark 1:3; Isa. 40:3-11). John, the promised messenger, has prepared the way (John 1:2-4). Jesus announces, "The time is fulfilled, and the kingdom of God is at hand" (Mark 1:15, RSV). He comes for baptism, is anointed by the Holy Spirit, and is hailed by the Father as his promised Son (1:11). He will baptize with the Holy Spirit (1:8). Jesus is filled with power and wisdom as revealed in his works and words. Throughout, Jesus is the suffering Son of man (8:31).

Mark is a Gospel *in a hurry*. Jesus is on the move. A favorite word is the Greek word *euthus*, meaning *immediately* or *at once*, or *then*. It occurs about forty times.

Mark is also characterized by *amazement* and *holy fear*. Seven times the disciples are *amazed* by Jesus's actions (1:27; 2:12; 6:51; 9:15; 10:32; 14:33; 16:8). At least five times they are seized by fear (*phobeo*; 4:41; 5:15; 6:50; 9:6; 16:8). In the events of Jesus's life and death, God has at last torn open (1:10; 15:38, σχίζω, *schizo*, "to cleave, sever") the heavens and come down. In him, judgment and restoration have come upon Israel in a way anticipated in Scripture.[38]

The story of Jesus is presented as a secret or mystery to be penetrated by faith alone. Jesus, the crucified Messiah, is the mystery, enfolded in apocalyptic urgency. Mark relentlessly concentrates on the cross and concludes on a note of hushed and puzzling hope.[39]

37. Bauckham, *Jesus and the Eyewitnesses*, xii.
38. Hays, *Echoes of Scripture*, 19.
39. Hays, *Reading Backwards*, 17.

Mark does not blurt out the mystery. Instead, he circumspectly conceals it in figures, riddles, and whispers.[40] Mostly he accomplishes his narrative magic through hints and allusions. He offers just enough clues to enlist readers in additional exploration and reflection. Sometimes Mark steps from behind the curtain and calls attention to an important intertextual allusion (e.g., "Let the reader understand" [13:14]). Mostly, his biblical references are woven into the story's fabric.[41]

Mark gradually unveils the mystery surrounding Jesus's identity by drawing upon Israel's Scripture. Four christological themes emerge: (1) Jesus as the Davidic King; (2) Jesus as the Son of Man; (3) Jesus as the embodied presence of the God of Israel; and (4) Jesus as the crucified Messiah.[42] Mark unites these themes in an astonishing but coherent portrayal.[43]

Mark anticipates Jesus's suffering (the climax of Mark's narrative) by three increasingly explicit predictions (8:31; 9:31; 10:33-34). In each instance, Jesus's disciples misunderstand (8:32; 9:33-34; 10:35-37). Mark interprets the events surrounding Jesus's passion not as the death of a sinner cursed by God but as the Son of God (1:11) who understands and embraces his divine mission in light of Scripture. Jesus dies in radical obedience to his Father.[44] He declares, "Not what I will, but what you will" (14:36, NIV). Mark also understands Jesus's death as radical service to humanity: "This is my blood of the covenant, which is poured out for many" (v. 24).

The scandal of Jesus's death is not denied. He is fearful before he suffers. He chooses not to defend himself before his accusers, is mocked and scourged, betrayed by one disciple, denied by another, and abandoned by them all. Mark calls readers to contemplate a paradoxical revelation that "shatters our categories and exceeds our understanding."[45]

---

40. Ibid., 62-64.
41. Ibid.
42. Ibid., 45-46.
43. Ibid., 46.
44. L. T. Johnson, *The Real Jesus*, 153.
45. Hays, *Echoes of Scripture*, 103.

## Luke

In his two-volume work (Luke-Acts), Luke narrates God's actions as he fulfills the promise of redemption made to Israel. The saving power of God in overflowing fullness has arrived. Fulfilling the prophetic promise of *shalom* (peace) is the goal of God's liberating activity.[46] Luke demonstrates this through a coherent *dramatic epic* that extends from Adam (3:38), through Abraham to Jesus, and into the church's life.[47]

As Luke tells the story, the Old Testament is largely composed of covenant promises God made to Israel. The first two chapters recall these promises. God has joined himself to this particular people; he can be trusted to rescue them from oppression. The concluding resurrection appearances confirm that all promises made have been fulfilled in Jesus.[48] Fulfillment continues in the life of the church. In the Spirit's power, the church will serve and glorify God in holiness and righteousness.[49]

According to Luke, Jesus is Israel's Lord and God. This narrative foundation explains and integrates Luke's accounts.[50] Jesus Messiah is *Kyrios*, Lord of all.[51] His identity "unfolds *cumulatively* throughout the Gospel."[52] He possesses authority to forgive sins (5:18-26; 7:48), asserts sovereignty over Sabbath restrictions (6:1-16), and commands the forces of nature (8:22-25). As promised by Isaiah (Isa. 61:1-2; 58:6), Jesus redeems the poor and downtrodden (Luke 4:16-19).

Jesus's word demonstrates authority because it is the word of God that transcends human mortality and creation's limitations (Luke 21:32-33).[53] He shares/embodies "the identity and presence of Israel's God."[54] He confers powers and blessings only God can confer. He can appoint disciples and give them authority over demons and diseases (9:1-2; 10:19). He can promise and then fulfill the outpouring of the Holy Spirit—a prerogative

---

46. Ibid., 200.
47. Ibid., 192.
48. Ibid., 193.
49. Ibid., 200.
50. Ibid., 243.
51. Ibid., 353.
52. Ibid., 244.
53. Ibid., 256.
54. Ibid.

belonging exclusively to God (24:29; Acts 2:33).[55] The weeping figure who approaches Jerusalem and prophesies its destruction (19:41-44) is not some disappointed prophet. He is the one in whom God's judging and saving visitation is enacted.[56]

Luke's distinctive literary features serve his overall purposes: (1) emphasis on the fulfillment of prophecy and the spirit of prophecy in the church. Throughout the Gospel, Jesus identifies himself with Israel's heroes—especially Moses, but also the prophets Elijah and Elisha. Jesus articulates his sense of divine mission in words borrowed from Isaiah (Luke 4:16-30); (2) development of a prophetic Christology and model of authority; and (3) use of the story of Moses for structuring Luke and Acts.

Luke is a masterful storyteller who can in a few words generate a world. In Acts, his stories range from the humor of Rhoda dithering at the gate (12:12-17), the irony of the secret and sacred Sanhedrin session (5:33-39), and to Paul addressing philosophers in Athens (17:16-34). Luke includes exquisite parables of compassion and mercy, such as the prodigal son (15:11-24) and the Good Samaritan (10:30-35).

Luke teaches his audience who they are and how they are to live.[57] He draws a direct line from the risen Christ to the infant community of Christian believers. The Christian community is *continuous* with Israel of old, God's ancient purposes, and the church's validation as God's people.

Richard Hays concludes his exposition of Jesus's identity in Luke's Gospel by observing that the hope placed in Jesus as Israel's Redeemer was fulfilled in richer ways than the two dispirited disciples walking to Emmaus (24:13) could have imagined.

He redeems Israel as the Spirit-anointed Servant who announces liberation and leads Israel on a new exodus; he redeems Israel as the royal Davidic Messiah who redefines and restores the promised kingdom through his own suffering and vindication; he redeems Israel as the prophet who, like Elijah and Elisha, works healing miracles and unsettles corrupt power.[58]

---

55. Ibid., 261-62.
56. Ibid., 258.
57. Ibid.
58. Ibid., 262-63.

He is the Lord (*Kyrios*, YAHWEH embodied), the Redeemer of Israel and light to the nations (Luke 2:32).[59]

# John

John prefaces and accompanies his work by announcing that in Jesus "the Word" (1:1) all Old Testament prophecies and expectations have been fulfilled. The "Word" is both Creator and Redeemer (vv. 1-5). Jesus's coming into the world must consequently be understood as inaugurating a new age, and a new order of relations between God and humankind. This is confirmed by appealing to the presence of the Spirit in the church.

In his classic commentary on the Gospel of John, Welsh New Testament scholar C. H. Dodd (1884—1973) says, "There is no book, either in the New Testament or outside it, which is really *like* the Fourth Gospel."[60] In it we encounter the work of "a powerful and independent mind."[61] Historian of Christian doctrine Adolph Harnack adds that John "clothes the indescribable with words."[62]

The fourth gospel has traditionally been attributed to John, the son of Zebedee, the disciple "whom Jesus loved" (John 13:23; see Matt. 10:2; Mark 3:17; and Luke 5:4). St. Irenaeus (c. 130-c. 202) says John lived and wrote at Ephesus.[63] Or John the Elder could have been the author. Wright and Bird "cautiously" vote for John the elder, a Judean disciple of Jesus, not one of the Twelve.[64] Because the Gospel never mentions a "John" other than John the Baptist, none of this is certain. According to Richard Bauckham, it is certain that an eyewitness wrote John.[65]

No matter who the author was, the fourth gospel "stands today as it has for two thousand years as a coherent, profound, and challenging wit-

59. Ibid., 253-62.

60. C. H. Dodd, *The Interpretation of the Fourth Gospel* (Cambridge, UK: Cambridge University Press, 1970), 6.

61. Ibid.

62. Adolph Harnack, *History of Dogma*, Vol. I (New York: Dover Publications, 1900), 96-97.

63. Irenaeus, *Adversus Haereses* [*Against Heresies*], bk. 3, chap. 1. New Advent. http://www.newadvent.org/fathers/0103301.htm.

64. N. T. Wright and Bird, *The New Testament in Its World*, 659.

65. Bauckham, *Jesus and the Eyewitnesses*, 6.

ness, itself sufficient evidence that the [Christian community in which John was written] had within it one great theologian and writer."[66]

Two features illustrate the Gospel's artistry. *First*, the use of irony as a literary technique: Readers always know more than the participants in the narrative and are able to appreciate words and actions at a different level. Characters are given lines that state truths beyond their own intentions (e.g., 11:50).[67] Almost everything in John has a symbolic value, including names (1:42, 47; 9:7) and numbers (2:1, 6; 6:13, 70; 21:11). *Second*, the book has four well-defined major parts: (1) the prologue (1:11-18); (2) the Book of Signs (1:19—12:50); (3) the Book of Glory (13:1—20:31) (ironically, Christ's "glory" is his crucifixion, his "lifting up" [12:32]); and (4) an epilogue (21:1-25).

Unlike Matthew, Mark, and Luke, John uses *signs* (*semeia*) to speak of Jesus's miracles. Jesus performs seven signs corresponding to the seven days of the new creation. They are the wedding at Cana (2:1-11); healing the official's son (4:46-53); healing the paralytic (5:2-9); multiplying the loaves (6:1-13); walking on water (6:16-21); healing the man born blind (9:1-12); and raising Lazarus from the dead (11:17-44). The signs manifest Jesus's identity as the one who acts by God's authority. He is the "living water" (4:10), the "bread of life" (6:35), the "light of the world" (8:12), and the "resurrection and the life" (11:25). The signs point to the unity between Jesus's work and the work of the Father. They demonstrate that in Jesus, full disclosure of God's glory and grace are occurring. If correctly received, the signs lead to faith and eternal life.

For John, Jesus is above all the definitive revelation of God (1:14, 18) who has come at last to rescue, heal, and feed his people (Ezek. 34:15-16).[68] He is eternal (John 1:2). He is God incarnate, for in him YAHWEH has "pitched his tent [*tabernacled*] among us" (v. 14, AT). Jesus manifests God's glory in the world (v. 14; Heb. *kabod*; Gr. *doxa*). He does what only God can do: create the world (vv. 2-3). Moses and the prophets wrote about him (v. 45; 5:46). Still, in John there are times when Jesus appears

---

66. L. T. Johnson, *The Writings*, 466.
67. Ibid., 472.
68. Hays, *Echoes of Scripture*, 320.

to be even more human than in the Synoptics (2:4; 4:6; 6:26; 7:1-10; 8:25; 11:33-35; 12:7; 13:21).

John "captures the whole drama of God's relationship with humanity, and Jesus is the central character."[69] He emphasizes Jesus's "otherness," his "deity" in astonishing ways. Jesus is none other than the *enfleshed* "I am" (8:58). He speaks as "no man ever spoke" (7:46, RSV). The "glory" Jesus seeks is that of the Father who sent him (7:18; 8:50, 54; 9:24; 11:4, 40; 12:28, 43; 13:31). He is the obedient Son who speaks only as his Father directs (8:26-28) and works only as he sees his Father working (5:10, 17).

The supreme "work of God" happens in Jesus's passion and death where he is "lifted up" (12:32). Astonishingly, Jesus's death is the supreme revelation of God's love and glory. Paradoxically, the crucifixion manifests God's *effective* presence in the world (cf. 7:39; 12:16, 23, 28; 13:31; 17:5), a presence known not by human wisdom but in "new birth" (3:1-15) and the *convincing witness* of the Holy Spirit (15:26-27; 16:4*b*-11).

For outsiders, Jesus's death is that of a victim who could do nothing to avert his "deserved" fate (5:18; 6:64; 7:1; 8:15). But for insiders, Jesus's death is a willing sacrifice for the sake of others. He dies "for the nation, and not for the nation only, but to gather into one the children of God who are scattered abroad" (11:51-52, RSV). Jesus is the Good Shepherd who willingly lays down his life for the sheep (10:11, 15). When on the cross, from his side "water came out" (19:34), outsiders see a helpless Roman victim. By faith, insiders see a symbol of the Holy Spirit being given (v. 30), the one whom "those who believed in him were to receive" (7:39, RSV).

Wright and Bird conclude their riveting account of the fourth gospel by saying if we hear John correctly, then by the Spirit we will comprehend that for all humankind, the Creator who became lovingly incarnate in that which he created "is the door between our world and the new creation."[70] Wright suspects the whole Gospel is about creation and new creation. New creation involves complete renewal of the old, not its abolition, now that "the ruler of this world" is being "cast out" (12:31, RSV).[71]

---

69. L. T. Johnson, *The Real Jesus*, 156.
70. N. T. Wright and Bird, *The New Testament in Its World*, 678.
71. N. T. Wright, *History and Eschatology*, 264.

According to John, Christ is not just one option on a religious buffet. He is singularly the "bread of life" (6:35). He is not one *way* up the mountain, among others. In the beginning he created the mountain! (1:3). Jesus Christ is the world's Creator and Redeemer, the truth, and the life for all. John bids us embrace the all-exclusive claims of the all-inclusive Savior.[72] However, counsels Benedict XVI, according to the Fourth Evangelist, who Christ *is*—grace and truth incarnate—can be known only through the Holy Spirit. John is a "pneumatic Gospel."[73]

## Conclusion

In opening his *Evangelii gaudium* [The Joy of the Gospel] Pope Francis exults, "The joy of the gospel fills the hearts and lives of all who encounter Jesus. Those who accept his offer of salvation are set free from sin, sorrow, inner emptiness, and loneliness. With Christ, joy is constantly born anew."[74]

"The joy of the gospel" as *good news* for all constitutes the four Gospels. At Jesus's birth, angels announced to startled shepherds "good news of great joy" (Luke 2:10). Upon learning of Jesus's resurrection, the two Marys, filled with joy, run to tell Jesus's dejected disciples (Matt. 28:8). Jesus told his disciples his own joy would be in them (John 15:11). Rejoice! In Jesus's cross and resurrection, God has defeated the powers that enslaved the world, and launched the new creation (Eph. 1:9-10; Col. 2:13-15).

Now, the joyous mission of God through his church is to demonstrate the gospel's life-transforming power, and to call all people to participate in God's new creation.

72. N. T. Wright and Bird, *The New Testament in Its World*, 678.

73. Benedict XVI, *Jesus of Nazareth*, 232-35.

74. Francis, *Evangelii gaudium* [The Joy of the Gospel]. Vatican Website. November 24, 2013. http://www.vatican.va/content/francesco/en/apost_exhortations/documents/papa-francesco _esortazione-ap_20131124_evangelii-gaudium.html#The_joy_of_the_gospel.

# 13

# PAUL AND THE FULFILLED PROMISES OF GOD

Through careful study, present-day scholars have produced a rich under-standing of Paul's life and ministry. N. T. Wright's *Paul: A Biography* helps us understand "what made Paul tick."[1]

Paul the apostle was born early in the first century in Tarsus, capital city of the ancient Roman province of Cilicia. Saul was his Hebrew name, Paul his Latin name. The custom of dual names was common. Though both names are used in Acts, he became best known as Paul. He inherited Roman citizenship because his father was a Roman citizen. His family belonged to the Pharisee party. They were engaged in the tent making business.

Paul was raised with a keen familiarity with the Scriptures. He seems to have "swallowed the Bible whole."[2] He matured in an atmosphere of religious story and symbol. The story was awaiting its divine fulfillment

---

1. N. T. Wright, *Paul: A Biography* (New York: HarperOne, 2018), 10.
2. Ibid., 16.

(Acts 26:4-8). A complex of symbols gave it coherence and enabled Jews to live in it.[3]

Wright describes Paul as energetic and talkative, but physically unattractive.[4] He was among the most intellectually capable of the first century, unsurpassed by the likes of Seneca, Plutarch, and a small band of others.[5] He read biblical Hebrew fluently, spoke Aramaic, wrote and spoke in Greek, and probably knew some Latin. He was familiar with the ideas of the non-Jewish philosophers of his day. His "great learning" was known among his opponents (Acts 26:24).

Most likely during Paul's teen years, he went to Jerusalem to become a student of Gamaliel the Elder, one of the great rabbis of that period. As a young man, Paul became a prominent figure among the Pharisees (cf. Acts 26:4-8).

## The Story Awaiting Fulfillment

The story by which Paul lived was rooted in creation and covenant. Jews, children of Abraham, were chosen *from* the world, but also *for* the world. Israel was meant to be a light to the Gentiles (Isa. 49:6), the people through whom all nations would be blessed. They had once been rescued from Egyptian slavery. The One God had made a covenant with them in a relationship that could be temporarily, but never permanently, fractured.[6]

The single great Jewish story was grounded in Genesis and Exodus, in Abraham and Moses. Though Israel had been called to worship the One God alone, it had failed badly. As a result, in 587 BC Israel had been exiled to Babylon. The young Saul would have seen the connection between Adam and Eve being exiled from the garden of Eden (Gen. 3:22-24) and Israel being exiled from the promised land. The Israelites had worshipped idols. So they had been "expelled" to Babylon.

One prophet after another announced that a covenantal separation had occurred. God had abandoned the temple to destruction by foreigners

---

3. Ibid., 17.
4. Ibid., 1.
5. Ibid., 112.
6. Ibid., 18.

and permitted the exile. The abandonment began a long, puzzling interval between the start of exile (587 BC) and when the One God would return in glory. Heaven and earth would come together as promised.

Many Jews read the scriptures as teaching that exile—theologically and politically—had not ended. It was "a state of mind and heart, of politics and practicalities, of spirit and flesh."[7] Deuteronomy, Isaiah, Jeremiah, and Ezekiel looked forward to a great restoration and fulfillment of Israel's calling. Under various leaders, some Jews had returned to Jerusalem, and the temple had been restored (516 BC). But neither the rebuilt temple nor the physical return conformed to the promised restoration.

The books of Ezra and Nehemiah sounded out the complaint, "We have returned to our own land. But we are still slaves. We are ruled by a foreign power."[8] "Slaves" need a new exodus such as Isaiah had promised.

This was the hope: that the story at the heart of the Five Books [Genesis-Deuteronomy]—slavery, rescue, divine presence, promised land—would spring to life once more as the answer *both* to the problem of covenantal rebellion in Deuteronomy 27—32 *and* to the parallel, and deeper, problem of human rebellion in Genesis 1—3. The former would be the key to the latter: when the covenant God did what he was going to do for Israel, then somehow—who knew how?—the effects would resonate around the whole world.[9]

Many forward-looking Jews like young Saul—soaked in scriptures such as Daniel and Deuteronomy—were eager for the long-delayed divine deliverance (resurrection),[10] the final saving revelation. By their interpretation of Daniel 9 they figured the exile would last almost half a millennium. Afterward, God would finally deal with the sins that had caused the exile. Many, Saul included, believed the time for deliverance, the end of exile, was near. Strict obedience to the Torah and defense of the temple were urgent. Failure to be faithful could postpone the final deliverance. This partly explains why Saul, zealous (Gal. 1:14) for the Law and temple,

7. Ibid., 46.
8. Ibid., 19.
9. Ibid.
10. Michael J. Gorman, *The Death of the Messiah and the Birth of the New Covenant* (Eugene, OR: Cascade Books, 2014), 43.

vigorously persecuted Jesus's followers. He believed they were blasphemously obstructing fulfillment of God's promises.

For many Jews living outside Palestine, even though the Jerusalem temple remained central, the Torah served as a movable temple. Geographically and symbolically the temple was where heaven and earth meet. It signaled fulfillment of the ultimate promise, the renewal and unity of heaven and earth. The temple signaled hope for a new creation where God would be forever present. It was like a cultural and theological magnet, bringing together heaven and earth, and all the great biblical stories and expectations.[11] Prophets had promised that one day, to this focal point of Israel's hope, the One God would return in all of his radiant presence and power.[12] Isaiah foretold (Isa. 52:7-12; cf. Ezek. 43:1-27; Mal. 3:1) Jerusalem would be redeemed and the One God would establish his kingdom in visible power and glory. After Isaiah's promise, no Jewish writers claimed God had returned in glory to his temple.[13]

Israel's story of exodus and freedom described God's past actions. And it was the story of what God would do again: a new, second exodus, bringing full and final freedom. The anticipated future was firmly secured in unshakable divine promise. The Covenant Keeper's faithfulness is his *righteousness* (Heb. *tsedaqah elohim*; Gr. *dikaiosyne theou*). Neither Adam being exiled from Eden, nor Israel being exiled to Babylon could be the story's conclusion. Otherwise, the One God would have committed gross failure.

In the words of New Testament scholar Andrew K. Boakye, who agrees with Wright's treatment of exile, Israel "was hovering on the cusp" of a profound second exodus.[14]

---

11. N. T. Wright, *Paul: A Biography*, 20.

12. Ibid., 21.

13. Ibid. N. T. Wright says we will never understand how the young Saul of Tarsus thought and prayed "until we grasp the strange fact that, though the Temple still held powerful memories of divine presence (as does Jerusalem's Western Wall to this day for [many] Jews . . . who . . . do not think that the One God actually resides there now), there was a strong sense that the promise of ultimate return had not yet been fulfilled" (ibid.).

14. Andrew K. Boakye, *Death and Life: Resurrection, Restoration, and Rectification in Paul's Letter to the Galatians* (Eugene, OR: Pickwick, 2017), 5. Boakye cites Philip Alexander, former head of Jewish Studies at the University of Manchester, as strongly supporting Wright's view of Second Exodus expectation, 11.

# The Crisis

Saul was angry! A self-styled Galilean prophet, not much older than Saul, had caused considerable disturbance in the temple. He had taken it upon himself to drive out those he believed to be abusing the temple. He had claimed authority as the Messiah. By Saul's reckoning, the action was totally out of order. Finally, the authorities had arrested the troublemaker and handed him over to the Romans who killed him in the most shameful way imaginable—crucifixion. "Don't mess with Rome" was the message. That troublemaker's cruel death proved he was a blaspheming imposter. No one had ever heard of a crucified Messiah (cf. Deut. 21:22-23). The mere idea was a contradiction in terms, scandalous for Jews and foolishness for Gentiles (1 Cor. 1:23).

Astonishingly, that troublemaker's followers were claiming God had raised him from the dead! They spoke as though heaven and earth had already been joined in him. They claimed that with his resurrection new creation had begun! They claimed the temple was only of temporary, anticipatory importance. They declared the present generation stood under divine judgment for rejecting Jesus as Messiah.

Stephen, a follower of Jesus, had made matters worse by shouting, "Look, . . . I see heaven open and the Son of Man standing at the right hand of God" (Acts 7:56, NIV). Because of his "blasphemy," Stephen was rushed out of the city and stoned. Saul watched him die and approved (7:58—8:1).

Being cautious, some of Jesus's followers then abandoned Jerusalem and scattered throughout Judea and Samaria (Acts 8:1). Wherever they went, they echoed Stephen's declaration. They displaced ancient Israelite symbols, including the temple, by placing Jesus at the center. Meanwhile, Saul was "ravaging the church" by having Christians placed in prison (Acts 8:3; 26:9-11).

He believed the sins that provoked the Babylonian exile were egregious. But these Jesus followers were even worse. If permitted to continue, they could easily bring down God's wrath upon the people. Saul knew what the darkening crisis required. He sat out as a new Phinehas who once impaled a Midianite woman and her Israelite lover (Num. 25:6-9), and as a new Elijah who opposed idolatrous King Ahab (1 Kings 18:1-19) in defense of Torah and singular worship. The one true God was under attack. "With his Bible in his head, zeal in his heart, and official documents from the chief priests in his hand, young Saul set off [for Damascus] in the firm hope that he too would be recognized as a true covenant member."[15]

## The Encounter

On his way to Damascus, Saul was confronted. "Suddenly a light from heaven flashed around him. He fell to the ground and heard a voice say to him, 'Saul, Saul, why do you persecute me?' 'Who are you, Lord?' Saul asked. 'I am Jesus, whom you are persecuting,' he replied. 'Now get up and go into the city, and you will be told what you must do'" (Acts 9:3-6, NIV; see 26:12-18).

The zealous-for-the-Torah Saul had come face-to-face with Jesus of Nazareth.[16] He had been arrested by the One God whom he had worshipped and served all his life![17]

Saul was shaken to his core. The encounter "shattered his wildest dreams and, at the same spilt second, fulfilled them."[18] Jesus, Saul now realized, was the shocking fulfillment of Israel's ancient scriptures, but also the complete rejection of how Paul had been reading them.[19]

## Interpreting the Encounter

This encounter with the risen Christ gave Paul the key for interpreting his formidable knowledge of Judaism. Now he would comprehensively articulate the meaning of Jesus as the promised Messiah (*Christos*) of God (e.g., Acts 26:14-23; Rom. 15:7-13). His message about Jesus, God, and the

---

15. N. T. Wright, *Paul: A Biography*, 39.

16. Ibid., 52. For a twenty-first-century account similar to what Paul experienced, see Dikkon Eberhart, "Crossing the Road to Christ," *Christianity Today* (December 2019), 71-72.

17. N. T. Wright, *Paul: A Biography*, 52.

18. Ibid.

19. Ibid., 53-54. We must recognize that many Jews, if not most, completely reject the claim of such "fulfillment." The late leading Jewish scholar Jacob Neusner articulated the rejection, "The conception of a Judeo-Christian tradition that Judaism and Christianity share is simply a myth in the bad old sense: a lie" (*Jews and Christians: The Myth of a Common Tradition* [Eugene, OR: Wipf and Stock, 2003], preface).

world would be creative, compelling, and controversial. In proclaiming the gospel, he would announce what it means to be truly human[20] and truly Israel. Paul's proclamation was founded on the conviction that Jesus's prayer for God's kingdom to come "on earth as in heaven" (Matt. 6:10) had come to birth. Its inauguration was now being enacted by the Spirit.[21]

Paul realized that in Jesus Christ there had occurred "the *coming together* of heaven and earth . . . in a great act of cosmic renewal."[22] "The drama of Paul's career," Wayne A. Meeks concurs, "turns on his recognition that [the story of God's Son] shattered and recreated his own conception of a life lived in obedience of God's will. . . . For him [the story] equally shattered and recreated—but preserved!—Israel's fundamental reason for existing in the world as God's people."[23]

In history, in the real world of space, time, and matter, in Jesus of Nazareth, God had launched a heaven-and-earth movement.[24] The messianic age had dawned, restoration from exile had arrived, and the new covenant people of God had come to birth.[25] This had always been God's plan. The "good news" of the Messiah opened for Paul a new world, a new creation, in which everything true, beautiful, and pleasing would be at home.[26] Paul knew he was living at the final turning point of history.[27] "God the Creator had raised Jesus from the dead, declaring not only that he really was Israel's Messiah, but that he had done what the One God had prom-

---

20. N. T. Wright, *Paul: A Biography*, 1. Benedict XVI calls our attention to the fact that in nascent Christian faith there are two types of confessional formulas: the *substantive* and the *verbal*, one *ontological*, the other *salvation history*. Peter's confession, "You are the Messiah, the Son of the living God" (Matt. 16:16) is *substantive*. The long prophetic expectation found in the *history of salvation* constitutes the *verbal* confession. "Without the concrete history of salvation, Christ's titles remain ambiguous." But the history of salvation, apart from "the mystery of the cross," leaves the *history of salvation* incomplete (Benedict XVI, *Jesus of Nazareth*, 298). The apostle Paul, as well as the apostle Peter, exits the unity of the *substantive* and the *verbal* confessions.

21. N. T. Wright, *Paul: A Biography*, 9.

22. Ibid., 8.

23. Wayne A. Meeks, *The Origins of Christian Morality: The First Two Centuries* (New Haven, CT: Yale University Press, 1993), 196.

24. N. T. Wright, *Paul: A Biography*, 9.

25. Boakye, *Death and Life*, 5.

26. N. T. Wright, *Paul: A Biography*, 17.

27. Ibid., 10.

ised to do himself, in person."[28] Devotion to Israel and the Torah had been laudable. But Paul had earlier misunderstood how God would fulfill his promises (cf. 2 Cor. 1:19-22). He had been wrong regarding Israel's vocation and identity. He had been wrong in his understanding of the Torah.

So, in the words of Richard Hays, believing "the gifts and the calling of God are irrevocable" (Rom. 11:29), his mind reshaped by the gospel (5:8), Paul began a fresh reading of Scripture. He saw "the whole mysterious drama of God's election of Israel . . . displayed as foretold *in Scripture itself*."[29] He, along with the other New Testament witnesses, saw that through the mysterious providence of God, the correspondence, the linkage between the Old and New Testaments reveals *"a divinely crafted pattern of coherence within the events and characters of the biblical narratives."*[30]

From now on, everything would focus on "the figure from whom there streamed a blinding light, the figure who addressed Paul as a master addresses a slave, the figure he recognized as the crucified Jesus of Nazareth."[31] This was God's Messiah. Temple and Torah were not ultimate realities. Instead, they were glorious signposts pointing to the new heaven-and-earth reality birthed in Jesus.[32] Paul realized that in Christ, by the Spirit, God's ancient promise to live with his people and to address them with his life-transforming word had been fulfilled.[33]

In the risen Christ, Paul encountered the reality toward which the temple had always pointed. God's glory had returned in its fullness (cf. John 1:14), but not as Paul and his fellow Jews had anticipated. As promised, God had done a "new thing" (Isa. 43:19). Subsequently, Paul rearranged his mind and redirected his life accordingly.

Paul uses astonishing temple language in a christological hymn. He tells the Colossian Christians that in Christ Jesus, "all the fullness of

---

28. Ibid., 53.

29. Hays, *Reading with the Grain of Scripture*, 397-99.

30. Ibid., 83.

31. N. T. Wright, *Paul: A Biography*, 53.

32. Ibid., 54. "Moses's Torah was given by God for a vital purpose, but that purpose was temporary, to cover the period before the fulfillment of the promise to Abraham. Now that this had happened, the Torah has no more to say on the subject. . . . If covenant membership were available through the Torah, the Messiah wouldn't have needed to die" (ibid., 159-60).

33. Ibid., 72.

God was pleased to dwell" (Col. 1:19; cf. Eph. 2:11-22). Paul has penned the highest possible description of Jesus. He has complemented John's announcement that "the Word became flesh and lived among us" (John 1:14).[34] Bringing heaven and earth together, in his shameful death, and resurrection, Christ has reconciled all things.[35] And the ten or twenty assorted Colossians gathered into Philemon's house were participants.[36]

Paul did not proclaim the beginning of a "new religion." In Galatians 6:16 he calls the church "the Israel of God." God never promised the Messiah would inaugurate a new religion. Neither did the Gentile churches view themselves that way.[37] Rather, Israel's God had fulfilled Israel's scriptures in ways no one had anticipated. In Christ, God "accomplishes all things according to the counsel of his will" (Eph. 1:11, RSV). The Christian faith expresses that "counsel" as fulfilment of Israel's hope and as good news for the whole world.

Paul remained fiercely loyal to Israel's God. As his letters reveal, his mission in the Greco-Roman world was on behalf of Israel's God. In the Spirit's power, he did his best to make plain what Moses and the prophets foretold, "that the Messiah would suffer and, as the first to rise from the dead, would bring the message of light to his own people and to the Gentiles" (Acts 26:23, NIV).[38] Paul understood loyalty to God and Israel's hope as loyalty to the crucified, risen, and ascended Christ, Israel's Messiah. Through him alone, and by trust in him, God's covenant faithfulness was being implemented. Those grasped by the gospel and empowered by the Spirit were being sent out as participants in the revealed *Missio Dei*.[39]

---

· 34. Ibid., 291.

35. Ibid.

36. Ibid.

37. Ibid., 340. Wright says Paul's point in Romans 11 "is not that Israel has been *replaced*, but that Israel has been *renewed* through the promised Messiah and the promised spirit, with Gentiles included, in similar prophetic fulfillment." He rebukes a "callous supersessionism that imagines that God called the Jews first but that, after they had rejected him, he washed his hands of them and transferred all their blessings and privileges to a Gentile-only church that would be a kind of 'replacement Israel'" (N. T. Wright and Bird, *The New Testament in Its World*, 381).

38. Ibid., 366.

39. N. T. Wright and Bird, *The New Testament in Its World*, 382.

Wright summarizes: For Paul, the gospel of the crucified and risen Christ "burned like a brand."[40]

## The Manifold Wisdom of God

Paul summarized the gospel as the revealed "manifold wisdom of God" (Eph. 3:10, NIV). The story of Israel had always been a rescue operation. Through Israel, God had intended to put humans and the whole world aright. Israel had needed more than a new Passover and a rescue from pagan tyrants. It needed forgiveness and new creation.[41] Then Israel—indeed the whole world—would be free at last. That had been the ancient hope Saul and his contemporaries had been living, the narrative, the hope nourished in their heads and hearts.[42]

Now in Christ, God had put the human project—the creation project—back on track, had done all he promised (2 Cor. 1:20). He had defeated death and launched new creation. Henceforth the words "God" and "Israel" would be understood with reference to what God accomplished *in person* in Jesus Messiah. Moreover, the risen Christ had commissioned Paul to found *"Jew-plus-Gentile communities, worshipping the One God in and through Jesus his son and in the power of the spirit."*[43] The promise to Abraham had been universalized—a worldwide Abrahamic family[44] centered in Jesus Christ as *Kyrios* who had won the victory over death, hell, sin, and the grave—all the powers that had enslaved the world and spawned idolatry and human wickedness.[45]

Paul saw that by the Spirit's power, the risen Christ was creating a new community that included all the nations. Gentiles were now free to worship the One God. Clearly, all impediments to Gentile inclusion in a new "sanctified" people had been abolished.

A new world order, "on earth as in heaven," had been launched. The world might not look very different; the old age was still rumbling on,

---

40. N. T. Wright, *Paul: A Biography*, 316.

41. Ibid., 47.

42. Ibid.

43. Ibid., 404.

44. Ibid., 74.

45. N. T. Wright says the powers "feed off idolatry" (ibid., 296).

though its power had been broken. The center of spiritual gravity had fundamentally shifted.[46] Christians must now reset their watches and learn to live "between the times."[47] They must announce in word and deed that everyone is invited to forgiveness and freedom from idolatrous oppression.

One day, this same Jesus will "descend from heaven" (1 Thess. 4:16) to consummate on earth God's inaugurated kingdom. In the "fulness of time" God will "unite [sum up] all things in [Christ], things in heaven and things on earth" (Eph. 1:10, RSV). God has made this known "in all wisdom and insight" (v. 9, RSV; see vv. 7-10). Even now, through the church, "the wisdom of God in its rich variety" is being made known "to the rulers and authorities in the heavenly places" (Eph. 3:10).

> *Proclaim to every people, tongue, and nation*
> *That God, in whom they live and move, is love;*
> *Tell how he stooped to save his lost creation,*
> *And died on earth that all might live above.*
> *Publish glad tidings, tidings of peace,*
> *tidings of Jesus, redemption, and release.*
> —Mary Ann Thompson, 1834—1923

---

46. Ibid., 78.
47. Ibid., 222.

# CONCLUSION

I have addressed the topic of this book while keenly aware that it conflicts with the spirit of religious pluralism, to say nothing of advanced secularism that hails the demise of "transcendence" and relegates all religions to fiction. This is nothing new. Confessing Jesus Christ as the definitive revelation of God and as sole Redeemer of the world has always been offensive to representatives of other visions of reality and perceptions of human flourishing. In our post-Enlightenment, postcolonial, and postmodern world, confessing Christ as Lord of all is probably more offensive than ever. Christians who continue to do so might be judged uninformed at best and bigoted at worst.

Similar charges accompanied the "scandal of the cross" the apostles and early church knowingly accepted in their proclamation of Jesus Messiah. They did this in a Greco-Roman world marked by a rich history of empire, philosophy, "religion," and culture. As has been true of apostolic faith through the centuries, the apostles affirmed Christ to be singularly the manifest power and wisdom of God (1 Cor. 1:24) because in him they redemptively encountered the creator and redeemer God. The encounter and its meaning made their confession compelling, convincing, and missional. For the church of Jesus Christ, that *reason for being* never changes.

The primary reason for confessing Christ as Lord of all can never be replaced by argument. However, the Christian faith can credibly provide a conceptual and historically informed account of why Christians make their confession. This book has attempted that. Remaining is how faithfully the church will confess its faith in word and deed, and whether the "offense" of its witness will derive from the faith itself or from misrepresentation of its Lord in any way.

Although it has not been our purpose to explain the relation between the Christian faith and other religions, we can confidently affirm that nowhere has God "left himself without a witness" (Acts 14:17; Rom. 1:19 20), and that Christ the Word of God is "the true light that gives light to everyone" (John 1:9, NIV). Along with hymn writer Frederick Faber, Christians proclaim, "There's a wideness in God's mercy, / like the wideness of the sea."[1] The free attracting activity of the Holy Spirit of God is perfectly consonant with Christ being the world's Redeemer.

Let the church be attentive to how the free Spirit of God is advancing the kingdom of the triune God toward its consummation.

---

1. Frederick W. Faber, "There's a Wideness in God's Mercy," in *Sing to the Lord* (Kansas City: Lillenas, 1993), no. 81.

# BIBLIOGRAPHY

❖ ❖ ❖

Achtemeier, Paul J., Joel B. Green, and Marianne Meye Thompson. *Introducing the New Testament: Its Literature and Theology*. Grand Rapids: Eerdmans, 2001.

"Ancient Jewish History: The Bar-Kokhba Revolt (132-135 CE)." Jewish Virtual Library. https://www.jewishvirtuallibrary.org/the-bar-kokhba-revolt-132-135-ce.

Anderson, Bernhard W. *Understanding the Old Testament*. 3rd ed. Englewood Cliffs, NJ: Prentice-Hall, 1975.

"Babylonian Talmud." British Library. https://www.bl.uk/collection-items/babylonian -talmud.

Barth, Karl. *Church Dogmatics*. Vol. 4, *The Doctrine of Reconciliation*, pt. 3.1. Translated by G. W. Bromiley. Edinburgh: T. and T. Clark, 2004.

Bauckham, Richard. *Bible and Mission: Christian Witness in a Postmodern World*. Grand Rapids: Baker Academic, 2003.

———. *Jesus and the Eyewitnesses: The Gospels as Eyewitness Testimony*. 2nd ed. Grand Rapids: Eerdmans, 2017.

———. *Jesus and the God of Israel: God Crucified and Other Studies on the New Testament's Christology of Divine Identity*. Grand Rapids: Eerdmans, 2008.

Benedict XVI (Joseph Ratzinger). *Deus caritas est* [God Is Love]. Vatican Website. December 25, 2005. http://www.vatican.va/content/benedict-xvi/en/encyclicals /documents/hf_ben-xvi_enc_20051225_deus-caritas-est.html.

———. *In the Beginning: A Catholic Understanding of the Story of Creation and the Fall*. Translated by Boniface Ramsey. Grand Rapids: Eerdmans, 1990.

———. *Jesus of Nazareth*. New York: Image Books, 2007.

———. *Truth and Tolerance: Christian Belief and World Religions*. Translated by Henry Taylor. San Francisco: Ignatius Press, 2004.

Boakye, Andrew K. *Death and Life: Resurrection, Restoration, and Rectification in Paul's Letter to the Galatians*. Eugene, OR: Pickwick, 2017.

Bond, Helen K. *The First Biography of Jesus: Genre and Meaning in Mark's Gospel.* Grand Rapids: Eerdmans, 2020.

———. *The Historical Jesus: A Guide for the Perplexed.* New York: T. and T. Clark, 2012.

Brown, Sherri. "'Follow Me': The Mandate for Mission in the Gospel of John." In *Cruciform Scripture: Cross, Participation, and Mission.* Edited by Christopher Skinner, Nijay Gupta, Andy Johnson, and Drew Strait. Grand Rapids: Eerdmans, 2021.

Buber, Martin. *On Judaism.* New York: Schocken Books, 1967.

———. *Tales of the Hasidim: The Early Masters.* New York: Schocken Books, 1970.

Coakley, Sarah. *Christ without Absolutes: A Study of the Christology of Ernst Troeltsch.* Oxford, UK: Clarendon Press, 1988.

Copan, Paul. *Is God a Vindictive Bully?: Reconciling Portrayals of God in the Old and New Testaments.* Grand Rapids: Baker Academic, 2022.

Dodd, C. H. *The Interpretation of the Fourth Gospel.* Cambridge, UK: Cambridge University Press, 1970.

Eberhart, Dikkon. "Crossing the Road to Christ." *Christianity Today,* December 2019.

Ehrman, Bart. *How Jesus Became God: The Exaltation of a Jewish Preacher from Galilee.* New York: HarperOne, 2014.

Faber, Frederick W. "There's a Wideness in God's Mercy." No. 81 in *Sing to the Lord.* Kansas City: Lillenas, 1993.

Flemming, Dean. *Foretaste of the Future: Reading Revelation in Light of God's Mission.* Downers Grove, IL: IVP Academic, 2022.

———. *Recovering the Full Mission of God: A Biblical Perspective on Being, Doing and Telling.* Downers Grove, IL: IVP Academic, 2013.

———. "Revelation Is Good News for Today, Not a Game Plan for the Future." *Christianity Today,* September 2022. https://www.christianitytoday.com/ct/2022/september/dean-flemming-revelation-prediction-missional-lens.html.

Francis (Jorge Bergoglio). *Evangelii gaudium* [The Joy of the Gospel]. Vatican Website. November 24, 2013. http://www.vatican.va/content/francesco/en/apost_exhortations/documents/papa-francesco_esortazione-ap_20131124_evangelii-gaudium.html#The_joy_of_the_gospel.

Gorman, Michael J. *Becoming the Gospel: Paul, Participation, and Mission.* Grand Rapids: Eerdmans, 2015.

———. *The Death of the Messiah and the Birth of the New Covenant.* Eugene, OR: Cascade Books, 2014.

Greggs, Tom. *The Breadth of Salvation: Rediscovering the Fullness of God's Saving Work.* Grand Rapids: Baker Academic, 2020.

"Halakhah: Jewish Law." Judaism 101. http://www.jewfaq.org/halakhah.htm.

Harnack, Adolph. *History of Dogma.* Vol. 1. New York: Dover Publications, 1900.

Hart, David Bentley. *Tradition and Apocalypse: An Essay on the Future of Christian Belief*. Grand Rapids: Baker Academic, 2021.

Hays, Richard B. *Echoes of Scripture in the Gospels*. Waco, TX: Baylor University Press, 2016.

————. *Reading Backwards: Figural Christology and the Fourfold Gospel Witness*. Waco, TX: Baylor University Press, 2014.

————. *Reading with the Grain of Scripture*. Grand Rapids: Eerdmans, 2020.

Hendriks-Kim, Eric. "Why China Loves Conservatives." *First Things*, January 2023.

Herberg, Will. *Judaism and Modern Man: An Interpretation of Jewish Religion*. Woodstock, VT: Jewish Lights, 1997.

Heschel, Abraham Joshua. *God in Search of Man: A Philosophy of Judaism*. New York: Farrar, Straus and Giroux, 1983.

Hick, John. *God and the Universe of Faiths*. 2nd ed. London: Oneworld, 2015.

Hick, John, and Paul F. Knitter, eds. *The Myth of Christian Uniqueness: Toward a Pluralistic Theology of Religions*. Eugene, OR: Wipf and Stock, 2004.

The Holy Qur'an. Translated by A. Yusuf Ali. https://quranyusufali.com/.

Irenaeus. *Adversus Haereses* [Against Heresies], bk. 3, chap. 1. New Advent. http://www.newadvent.org/fathers/0103301.htm.

Jenkins, Philip. *The Lost History of Christianity: The Thousand-Year Golden Age of the Church in the Middle East, Africa, and Asia—and How It Died*. New York: HarperOne, 2009.

Jenson, Robert W. *Visible Words: The Interpretation and Practice of Christian Sacraments*. Philadelphia: Fortress Press, 1978.

"The Jesus Seminar." Westar Institute. https://www.westarinstitute.org/projects/the-jesus-seminar/.

"Jihad: A Misunderstood Concept from Islam." Islamic Supreme Council of America. https://wpisca.wpengine.com/?p=9.

John Paul II (Karol Wojtyla). *Redemptor hominis* [The Redeemer of Man]. Vatican Website. March 4, 1979. http://www.vatican.va/content/john-paul-ii/en/encyclicals/documents/hf_jp-ii_enc_04031979_redemptor-hominis.html.

Johnson, Andy. "The Past, Present, and Future of Bodily Resurrection as Salvation: Christ, Church, and Cosmos." In *Cruciform Scripture: Cross, Participation, and Mission*. Edited by Christopher Skinner, Nijay Gupta, Andy Johnson, and Drew Strait. Grand Rapids: Eerdmans, 2021.

Johnson, Luke Timothy. *The Real Jesus: The Misguided Quest for the Historical Jesus and the Truth of the Traditional Gospels*. San Francisco: HarperSanFrancisco, 1996.

————. *The Writings of the New Testament: An Interpretation*. Minneapolis: Fortress Press, 2010.

Jones, Ryan. "Top Rabbis: Look at the Signs, Messiah Is Coming!" *Israel Today*, August 3, 2020. https://www.israeltoday.co.il/read/top-rabbis-look-at-the-signs-messiah-is-coming/.

Josephus, Flavius. *Antiquities of the Jews*, bk. 18, chap. 1.6. Early Jewish Writings. http://www.earlyjewishwritings.com/text/josephus/ant18.html.

———. *War of the Jews*, bk. 6, chap. 8.5. Early Jewish Writings. http://www.earlyjewish writings.com/text/josephus/war6.html.

"Kabbalah and Jewish Mysticism." Judaism 101. http://www.jewfaq.org/kabbalah.htm.

"Kabbalah: The Zohar." Jewish Virtual Library. https://www.jewishvirtuallibrary.org /the-zohar.

Kärkkäinen, Veli-Matti. *An Introduction to the Theology of Religions: Biblical, Historical and Contemporary Perspectives*. Downers Grove, IL: IVP Academic, 2003.

———. *Trinity and Religious Pluralism: The Doctrine of the Trinity in Christian Theology of Religions*. Burlington, VT: Ashgate, 2004.

Kaur, Valarie. *See No Stranger: A Memoir and Manifesto of Revolutionary Love*. New York: One World, 2020.

Kierkegaard, Søren. *Training in Christianity*. In *A Kierkegaard Anthology*. Edited by Robert Bretall. Princeton, NJ: Princeton University Press, 1946.

Knitter, Paul. *Introducing Theologies of Religions*. Maryknoll, NY: Orbis Books, 2002.

Lewis, C. S. *The Abolition of Man*. New York: Macmillan, 1947.

Mack, Burton L. *The Myth of Christian Supremacy: Restoring Our Democratic Ideals*. Minneapolis: Fortress Press, 2022.

Malina, Bruce J. *The New Testament World: Insights from Cultural Anthropology*. 3rd ed. Louisville, KY: Westminster John Knox Press, 2001.

Martyn, J. Louis. "A Personal Word." In Paul W. Meyer. *The Word in This World: Essays in New Testament Exegesis and Theology*. Edited by John T. Carroll. Louisville, KY: Westminster John Knox Press, 2004.

"Mashiach: The Messiah." Judaism 101. https://www.jewfaq.org/mashiach.htm.

McDermott, Gerald. *Can Evangelicals Learn from World Religions? Jesus, Revelation and Religious Transitions*. Downers Grove, IL: IVP, 2000.

Meacham, Jon. *The Hope of Glory: Reflections on the Last Words of Jesus from the Cross*. New York: Convergent Books, 2020.

Meeks, Wayne A. *The Origins of Christian Morality: The First Two Centuries*. New Haven, CT: Yale University Press, 1993.

Meyer, Paul W. *The Word in This World: Essays in New Testament Exegesis and Theology*. Edited by John T. Carroll. Louisville, KY: Westminster John Knox Press, 2004.

Murzaku, Ines A. "Persecuted and Forgotten? Defending Defenseless Christians." The Catholic Thing, December 28, 2019. https://www.thecatholicthing.org/2019 /12/28/persecuted-and-forgotten-defending-defenseless-Christians/?utm

_source=The+Catholic+Thing+Daily&utm_campaign=12e43d414d-EMAIL
_CAMPAIGN_2018_12_07_01_02_COPY_02&utm_medium=email&utm
_term=0_769a14e16a-12e43d414d-244109025.

"Muslims and Islam." Pew Research Center. https://www.pewresearch.org/fact-tank
/2017/08/09/muslims-and-islam-key-findings-in-the-u-s-and-around-the
-world/.

Netland, Harold. *Dissonant Voices: Religious Pluralism and the Question of Truth*. Vancouver, BC: Regent College Publishing, 1991.

———. *Encountering Religious Pluralism: The Challenge to Christian Faith and Mission*.
Downers Grove, IL: IVP Academic, 2001.

Neusner, Jacob. *Jews and Christians: The Myth of a Common Tradition*. Eugene, OR:
Wipf and Stock, 2003.

———. *A Rabbi Talks with Jesus*. Rev. ed. Montreal: McGill-Queen's University Press,
2000.

Newbigin, Lesslie. *The Gospel in a Pluralist Society*. Grand Rapids: Eerdmans, 1989.

Newman, John Henry. "General Answer to Mr. Kingsley." Pt. 7 of *Apologia Pro Vita Sua*
[A Defense of One's Own Life]. London: Oxford University Press, 1913. Christian Classic Ethereal Library. https://ccel.org/ccel/newman/apologia/apologia
.v.vii.html.

Noss, John B. *Man's Religions*. 7th ed. New York: Macmillan, 1984.

Novak, Philip. *The World's Wisdom: Sacred Texts of the World's Religions*. San Francisco: HarperSanFrancisco, 1994.

"Orthodox Judaism: Hassidism." Jewish Virtual Library. https://www.jewishvirtual
library.org/hasidism.

"The Path of Work: Karma Yoga." Vedanta Society of Southern California. https://
vedanta.org/yoga-spiritual-practice/the-path-of-work-karma-yoga/.

Percy, Walker. *The Message in the Bottle*. New York: Farrar, Straus and Giroux, 1975.

Perkins, Mckenzie. "Jainism Beliefs: The Five Great Vows and the Twelve Vows of
Laity." Learn Religions. https://www.learnreligions.com/jainism-beliefs-vows
-4583994.

Reimarus, Hermann Samuel. *Fragments from Reimarus*. Vol. 1. London and Edinburgh:
Williams and Northgate, 1879. Translated by G. E. Lessing. Edited by Charles Voysey. Internet Archive. https://archive.org/details/fragmentsfromrei00reim/page
/n3.

Rieff, Philip. *The Triumph of the Therapeutic: Uses of Faith after Freud*. New York:
Harper and Row, 1966.

Sacks, Jonathan. *A Letter in the Scroll: Understanding Our Jewish Identity and Exploring the Legacy of the World's Oldest Religion*. New York: Free Press, 2000.

Salkin, Jeffrey. "The Day Reform Judaism Made History." Religion News Service, March 24, 2021. https://religionnews.com/2021/03/24/israel-elections-reform -rabbi-gil-kariv/.

———. "Should Reform and Conservative Judaism Merge?" Religion News Service, May 19, 2020. https://religionnews.com/2020/05/19/reform-conservative -merger/.

Schiffman, Lawrence H. "The Second Temple." Bible Odyssey. https://www.bible odyssey.org/places/main-articles/the-second-temple/.

Schweitzer, Albert. *The Quest of the Historical Jesus: A Critical Study of Its Progress from Reimarus to Wrede.* Translated by W. Montgomery. London: Adam and Charles Black, 1911. Project Gutenberg. https://www.gutenberg.org/files/45422/45422 -pdf.pdf.

Scott, James M., ed. *Exile: A Conversation with N. T. Wright.* Downers Grove, IL: IVP Academic, 2017.

Shukla, Suhag. "What Does Hindutva Really Mean?" Hindu American Foundation, October 5, 2021. https://www.hinduamerican.org/blog/what-does-hindutva-mean.

Smith, Christian. *Religion: What It Is, How It Works, and Why It Matters.* Princeton, NJ: Princeton University Press, 2019.

Stone, Bryan. *Evangelism after Pluralism: The Ethics of Christian Witness.* Grand Rapids: Baker Academic, 2018.

The Tanakh. Jewish Virtual Library. https://www.jewishvirtuallibrary.org/the-tanakh -full-text.

*The Tao Te Ching,* I.1.1. Internet Archives. http://classics.mit.edu/Lao/taote.1.1.html.

Truesdale, Al, with Keri Mitchell. *With Cords of Love: A Wesleyan Response to Religious Pluralism.* Kansas City: Beacon Hill Press of Kansas City, 2006.

Wainwright, Geoffrey. *Doxology: The Praise of God in Worship, Doctrine, and Life.* New York: Oxford University Press, 1980.

Walton, John H. *Ancient Near Eastern Thought and the Old Testament.* Grand Rapids: Baker Academic, 2006.

Weigel, George. "The Easter Effect and How It Changed the World." *Wall Street Journal,* March 30, 2018. https://www.wsj.com/articles/the-easter-effect-and-how-it -changed-the-world-1522418701#comments_sector.

———. "Pope John Paul II's Soviet Spy." *Wall Street Journal,* May 14, 2020. https://www .wsj.com/articles/pope-john-paul-iis-soviet-spy-11589498606?mod=opinion _lead_pos10.

Wesley, John. "The Means of Grace." Sermon 16, pt. 5, sec. 4, in *The Sermons of John Wesley.* Wesley Center Online. http://wesley.nnu.edu/john-wesley/the-sermons-of -john-wesley-1872-edition/sermon-16-the-means-of-grace/.

"What in the World Is God Doing in Iran?" The Outreach Foundation, March 7, 2018. https://www.theoutreachfoundation.org/updates/2018/3/6/what-in-the-world -is-god-doing-in-iran.

"What Is a Fatwa?" Islamic Supreme Council of America. https://wpisca.wpengine .com/?p=106.

Wright, Christopher J. H. *The Mission of God: Unlocking the Bible's Grand Narrative.* Downers Grove, IL: IVP Academic, 2006.

Wright, N. T. *The Challenge of Jesus: Rediscovering Who Jesus Was and Is.* Downers Grove, IL: InterVarsity Press, 1999.

———. *The Day the Revolution Began: Reconsidering the Meaning of Jesus's Crucifixion.* San Francisco: HarperOne, 2016.

———. *History and Eschatology: Jesus and the Promise of Natural Theology.* London: SPCK, 2019.

———. *How God Became King: The Forgotten Story of the Gospels.* New York: Harper One, 2012.

———. *Jesus and the Victory of God.* Minneapolis: Fortress Press, 1996.

———. *Paul: A Biography.* New York: HarperOne, 2018.

———. *Paul in Fresh Perspective.* Minneapolis: Fortress Press, 2005.

———. *Surprised by Hope.* New York: HarperOne, 2008.

Wright, N. T., and Michael Bird. *The New Testament in Its World.* Grand Rapids: Zondervan Academic, 2019.

"The Zohar." The Kabbalah Centre, February 8, 2013. https://kabbalah.com/en /master-kabbalists/the-zohar.